CONTEND

CONTEND

Stewarding the Hearts and Destinies of our Children in Prayer

Margie Fleurant

Xulon Press
2301 Lucien Way #415
Maitland, FL 32751
407.339.4217
www.xulonpress.com

CONTEND
Stewarding the Hearts and Destinies of Our Children Through Prayer

© 2022 by Margie Fleurant

Cover Design by swinghousedesign.com

All rights reserved solely by the author. The author guarantees all contents are original and do not infringe upon the legal rights of any other person or work. No part of this book may be reproduced in any form without the permission of the author.

Due to the changing nature of the Internet, if there are any web addresses, links, or URLs included in this manuscript, these may have been altered and may no longer be accessible. The views and opinions shared in this book belong solely to the author and do not necessarily reflect those of the publisher. The publisher therefore disclaims responsibility for the views or opinions expressed within the work.

Unless otherwise indicated, Scripture quotations taken from the Holy Bible, New International Version (NIV). Copyright © 1973, 1978, 1984, 2011 by Biblica, Inc.™. Used by permission. All rights reserved.

Scripture quotations taken from the New King James Version (NKJV). Copyright © 1982 by Thomas Nelson, Inc. Used by permission. All rights reserved.

Scripture quotations taken from the Amplified Bible (AMP). Copyright © 1954, 1958, 1962, 1964, 1965, 1987 by The Lockman Foundation. Used by permission. All rights reserved.

Scripture quotations taken from the New American Standard Bible (NASB). Copyright © 1960, 1962, 1963, 1968, 1971, 1972, 1973, 1975, 1977, 1995 by The Lockman Foundation. Used by permission. All rights reserved.

Paperback ISBN-13: 978-1-6628-4763-9
eBook ISBN-13: 978-1-6628-4764-6

Dedication

To my children—Jonathan, Danielle, and Jaclyn. You taught me how to pray for you; now I get to pass on this knowledge and experience to others.

Table of Contents

Introduction	The Call to Fight	ix
Chapter 1	The Unexpected Route	1
Chapter 2	God's Value System	10
Chapter 3	Launching Our Arrows	21
Chapter 4	Training	27
Chapter 5	Prayer	33
Chapter 6	The Rising Generations: Millennials	41
Chapter 7	The Rising Generations: Generation Z	53
Chapter 8	The Elisha Company (Part 1)	62
Chapter 9	The Elisha Company (Part 2)	71
Chapter 10	Grace for Revival	81
Chapter 11	The Power to Pray	94
Chapter 12	Prayer Alerts	109
Chapter 13	Prayer Burdens	117
Chapter 14	The Warrior	127
Chapter 15	The Three Dimensions of Prayer	143
Chapter 16	Praying with Heaven's Mindset	159
Chapter 17	Practical Prayers for Our Children: Part 1	175
Chapter 18	Practical Prayers for Our Children: Part 2	193
	Conclusion	209
Appendix 1	More Sample Prayers	211
Appendix 2	Bible Promises for Our Children	217
	Endnotes	227

Introduction

The Call to Fight

> *Take delight in the LORD, and he will give you the desires of your heart. (Psalm 37:4)*

I have three children—all born in the same year. The story of their conception and birth are miraculous, and from the start, God spoke to me about my role as their mother, not just in the natural but in the spirit. When I birthed them physically, I stepped into another phase of motherhood in which I was the midwife called to help birth the destinies within my children.

God destined me to be a mother.

My Miraculous Journey to Motherhood

As parents, John and I decided to start trying to have children when I was thirty-three years old, but I had trouble conceiving. After a year, I went to see a fertility doctor, who ran some tests and performed a minor surgery on me to help my body be ready to conceive. Even this did not help. Unfortunately, there are many even in the Christian community who do not understand God's heart when it comes to couples facing difficulty conceiving.

Understanding God's Heart

The ability to bear children is a reward God has universally given to humanity as a sign of His love for us and His pleasure in us. When people have difficulty conceiving, it is not a curse from God. His will is for everyone to be able to bear children, just as it is His will for everyone to live in health. Thus, we must not see infertility as a lack of blessing, but as a need for healing. God's will for all married couples is to be able to have children.[1]

Intuitively, I had a sense I would have trouble with infertility, but that I would overcome it. He also told me that my first child would be a son (as well as some other details about him). So, from the very beginning, I had this perspective that I was in a fight against infertility, and I would overcome. I had been standing in faith on God's promise to me that I would become pregnant and would be a happy mother of children.

As part of this, I regularly prayed several verses out loud I believed aligned with God's will for my life and His call to be a mother.

> *Worship the* LORD *your God, and his blessing will be on your food and water. I will take away sickness from among you, and none will miscarry or be barren in your land. I will give you a full life span.* (Exodus 23:25–26)

> *There are three things that are never satisfied, four that never say, 'Enough!': the grave, the barren womb, land, which is never satisfied with water, and fire, which never says, 'Enough!'* (Proverbs 30:15–16)

> *The fruit of your womb will be blessed, and the crops of your land and the young of your livestock—the calves of your herds and the lambs of your flocks.* (Deuteronomy 28:4)

The Call to Fight

After reading these verses out loud, I would say, "Lord, I thank You that You said in Your Word You are not a man that You should lie and that all of Your promises are yes and amen (see Numbers 23:19, 2 Corinthians 1:20). I stand on Your Word, and I believe that my body is blessed. The fruit of my body is blessed, and by faith I am a happy mother of children. I thank You that You give me all the desires of my heart, and it is my desire to have children. I am blessed according to the Word of God, and so is the fruit of my body."

Although I had been standing in faith and confessing these promises, nothing was happening. Eventually, our doctor suggested we consider in vitro fertilization (IVF). This was a shock to me, because I had hoped and believed we would be able to conceive naturally. As a young girl, I remember seeing a news report about the first "test tube baby" and thinking, *A baby in a test tube?* Something about that moment left a huge impression on me, and the idea of undergoing IVF myself was unsettling. It was not what I wanted, yet I wanted children even more.

Chapter 1
The Unexpected Route

"For I know the plans I have for you," declares the LORD, *"plans to prosper you and not to harm you, plans to give you hope and a future."* (Jeremiah 29:11)

Though I agreed to it, I was not happy undergoing IVF. I had to give myself shots twice a day to help my body produce more eggs. Also, the cost of one IVF attempt was $5,000, and our insurance did not cover it. However, the biggest reason I was upset was because I could not understand why I wasn't getting pregnant naturally. I had been standing in faith, yet what I believed for was not happening. I couldn't wrap my mind around it, and it really shook my faith. Thankfully, God interrupted my confusion with a promise.

"For my thoughts are not your thoughts, neither are your ways my ways,: declares the Lord. "As the heavens are higher than the earth, so are my ways higher than your ways and my thoughts than your thoughts." (Isaiah 55:8-9)

One day, after a visit to the doctor, as I drove my car into the garage of our condo, God said to me, "You are going to have twins in your first pregnancy. You will get pregnant through in vitro fertilization." Then He said, "And in your second pregnancy you will conceive on your own."

I wrote His words down on a small yellow piece of paper I still have, tucked away in one of my journals. This gave me hope to persevere through the IVF cycle.

When it was time for us to go to the doctor for the retrieval of the eggs, the staff prepped me for the process and gave me a sedative to keep me comfortable.

After the doctor had retrieved four eggs, I sat up and said, "No more," meaning, "You can't have any more of my eggs."

Later, the doctor told me he'd never had anyone say that to him before. I'm not sure why I said it, but I believe the Holy Spirit inspired me.

After they gathered my eggs, they put them through the in vitro process, and from the four eggs, three embryos were produced. I still have a picture of my three precious embryos. These were miraculous results. When the time was right, the doctor implanted the three embryos in my womb, and I became pregnant in the first attempt. Two of the three embryos survived, and I found myself pregnant with twins, just like God had promised me.

I was overjoyed! I had clung to the promise that "Children are a heritage from the Lord" (Psalm 127:3).

Understanding God's Heart

*Behold, children are a **gift of the Lord**, the fruit of the womb is a reward. Like arrows in the hand of a warrior, so are the children of one's youth.* (Psalm 127:3–4 NASB emphasis added)

The word translated in Psalm 127 as "gift" can also be translated as "heritage." This is a word we don't use much today, but it carries an important added meaning. A *heritage* is an inherited possession, or an inheritance. In other words, it implies a legacy or an heirloom that is passed down through the generations. So, when God gives the gift of a child, He gives a piece of His legacy. He is adding to the family inheritance with the wealth of another child from His heart. Every child comes from the Father and is His possession (in the sense that He is the Creator and Sustainer).[2]

> **Every child is an heirloom in God's family, a valuable treasure that carries the essence of God's royal family line.**

At last, I was beginning to taste my reward. The moment I became a happy mother of children was one of the most joyous moments of my life. Nothing could compare to my previous sorrow when I could not conceive (see Proverbs 30:16), and now, nothing could compete with my joy. God had given me the desire of my heart, and finally I was pregnant. It was a miracle—to become pregnant at the first attempt at in vitro. Though the doctor played an important part, I recognized these babies were truly a miracle from God.

Further, the doctor decided to pay for our procedure himself and personally wrote us a check for $5,000. In His kindness, God had answered each one of my concerns about this process with signs of His goodness. He was with us every step of the way, and His blessing was manifesting in our lives—even if it wasn't in the way I had expected. We were thrilled. Our miracle was underway, and soon we would have the blessing of welcoming our babies into the world.

Pause and Reflect…

How has my testimony helped you understand God's heart for families?

Fighting for My Babies

As it turned out, we got to meet them much sooner than expected. When I was only twenty-eight weeks into the pregnancy, I started having contractions. This was not good. On top of that, I was also very sick because I had caught a virus. I started to go into pre-term labor, so the doctor gave me medication to stop the contractions and put me on complete bed rest for two weeks.

I remember while I was in pre-term labor and the doctor was measuring the contractions, my spirit stirred with indignation at what the devil was trying to do. John 10:10 says the devil comes to steal, kill, and destroy, but Jesus gives us abundant life. These babies were a good and perfect gift from God to me (see James 1:17). God had blessed me with them, and now the enemy had the audacity to try to steal them. This was not okay with me. It was time to keep fighting for my precious babies

Understanding Spiritual Warfare for Our Children

Jesus' mother Mary also faced attacks from the enemy trying to steal, kill, and destroy Jesus. God gave her and Joseph instructions to fight against these evil attacks. He will do the same for you and me as we keep fighting for our precious babies. Praying for our children from conception and throughout their lives is our responsibility as parents.

Two weeks later, on the evening before my baby shower, my contractions became stronger and more frequent. I could not get them to stop, and eventually I went into full-blown labor. I ended up missing my own baby shower because I was on the way to the hospital. When we reached the hospital, the staff gave me steroids to help with the development of the babies' lungs. They had done everything they knew to do to keep the babies inside, and now that it was becoming clear they were coming out anyway, they did all they could to help them survive. I was only thirty weeks and three days along, but ready or not, my babies were coming. The nurses prepped me for emergency surgery and wheeled me into the operating room.

The doctor began the C-section, and the first baby that came out of my womb was a boy—my son, Jonathan. This was exactly what God had promised me. Here's the funny thing. With twins, a C-section reverses the order. Baby A becomes Baby B because of the way the babies are delivered in a C-section. It is opposite to the way they would come out in a natural birth. This means, if I'd had them naturally, my daughter Danielle would have been born first instead of Jonathan. This realization comforted me greatly.

Even in this season of unexpected twists and turns, God had seen it all and His hand was on our lives. He was not thrown off by the devil's attack. Nothing could take Him by surprise.

So, Jonathan came out first, screaming loudly. After him came Danielle. It seemed she did not want to come out yet. I could feel her crawling up deep into my ribs, and it took the doctor a while to get her out. When he did lift her out, she made no noise, and the realization hit me like a hammer—*I need to fight for my children!*

I realized it was my job to contend for the hearts and destinies of my children, starting right then. God had given them to me as a gift and a reward, and His hand was on their lives. They had purpose and calling on their lives for this season in history, and it was my job to intercede for them. My awareness of my call as a praying, warring parent began that day, January 4, 1992, in the operating room.

Immediately I began to pray. I reminded God of the promises from His Word. I told Him, "You promised me I would be the happy mother of children. You promised me children are my reward. You promised me I would have twins in my first pregnancy."

Right there, while I was still on the operating table, I began the fight for my children, and I have never stopped fighting since.

At that hospital in Pennsylvania, I discovered that I was not simply birthing my children in the natural. I was also entering a life-long labor of watching and praying for my children to help birth them into their destiny. The work was not done when my physical labor ended. It was only beginning.

Not only did I have the responsibility to raise my children in the natural, but also, to fight for them in the spirit.

Jonathan and Danielle stayed in the hospital for the next six weeks. While their bodies grew, I fought for them in the spirit. God gave me verses for them, and I wrote those verses on their incubators. I declared the verses out loud over them, and I prayed for them in tongues.

Eventually, Jonathan reached 4.5 pounds, and I could have taken him home, but I waited until Danielle was also ready. I wanted us to all go home together. Finally, when Danielle was 4.5 pounds and Jonathan was 5 pounds, I took them both home. I had stayed with them in the hospital and learned how to care for them, so the hospital staff knew I was ready. Still, it was no easy task. Twins are a challenge, let alone premature twins. A 5-pound baby is so incredibly small, but we persevered, by the grace of God, and my little ones continued to grow.

Pause and Reflect…

> *Are you beginning to understand how important learning how to fight for your children is in God's plan for your family?*
>
> *How will that change your prayers for your children?*

Another Surprise

A few weeks after I brought Jonathan and Danielle home from the hospital, my best friend Marcia came to visit for a weekend. She had agreed to help take care of the babies so John and I could have a little break. Caring for one infant is a lot of work. Caring for two premature infants is even more, and we were worn out. Unbeknownst to any of us, that weekend I got pregnant again, naturally, when we least expected it. I had a baby growing inside me, and this time I didn't even know it.

Not long after that, I was at my friend Colleen's house for a playdate with several other mom friends and their kids. We always had a great time hanging out, enjoying our children, and fellowshipping with one another. It was a Godsend, having the support and encouragement from other moms. That particular time, as the four of us were sitting at the table, I suddenly had a strong feeling in my spirit that someone in the room was pregnant. I told them as much, but no one said it was her. I never even thought it could have been me.

A few weeks after that, I threw a party for the twins' dedication, and during the party I started to feel very sick. I thought I must have a virus. I felt sick to my stomach and very tired. In fact, I was so tired I actually fell asleep at my own party for the twins. I knew something was not right. I was craving orange juice, but I don't like orange juice! All the time I felt sick, I couldn't eat even though I was very thin.

When I went to the doctor, he asked if I was pregnant, and I told him that was impossible. So, he prescribed a medication and told me, "You cannot be pregnant and take this medication, because it's a medication that kills parasites."

I went home and started taking the medication. But after only a few doses, something on the inside of me said, "Stop taking the medication."

A few months went by, and I was feeling a bit better, so I stopped thinking about it and went on with life. I was so busy caring for the twins that I didn't have much time to really evaluate what might be happening. However, when the twins reached seven months of age, I started feeling something moving in my belly. I was so confused. What could it be? One night I pulled down the covers and watched it. Something was in there. It freaked me out. Was it possible I could be pregnant again?

With all of this churning inside me, I went to see my fertility doctor. Originally, I had scheduled the visit with him because I wanted him to see the twins, but now I had a pressing request. I told him what was going on.

"I don't feel well," I said. "Something's not right. Could you do a pregnancy test on me?"

"You're pregnant!" the doctor said, smiling at me.

He did an ultrasound. It was the most phenomenal thing I've ever seen in my life. On the screen, I saw my baby for the first time—a little girl with arms, legs, a head, and a body. I was already a full five months pregnant! With the twins, we had watched them grow from embryos and seen their development at every stage via ultrasound. Now, my little growing baby was already more than halfway developed.

Just nineteen weeks later, on Christmas Eve, 1992, Jaclyn was born. I had birthed three babies in one year. What a tremendous change and blessing in our lives all at once.

God had promised me that I would have three babies—two by IVF and one naturally—but He had never mentioned they would come all at once!

Understanding God's Heart

The Bible is full of stories of God coming through in impossible ways in impossible situations. It is His nature to be unhindered and unintimidated by human limitations. When the angel Gabriel appeared to Mary and told her she would become pregnant with the son of God, Mary asked how that could happen. It was truly impossible. Yet, Gabriel pointed to a higher reality. The person of the Holy Spirit and the power of the Most High could make even this "impossibility" possible (see Luke 1:34–35).

Gabriel ended his explanation to Mary with these comforting words: *"For no word from God will ever fail"* (Luke 1:37).

God's promises are good, and nothing is impossible to Him.

Chapter 2
God's Value System

*Behold, children are **a gift of the Lord, the fruit of the womb is a reward**. Like arrows in the hand of a warrior, so are the children of one's youth.* (Psalm 127:3–4 NASB emphasis added)

If we want to lead our children toward their destinies, the first step is renewing the way we see them to align with the way God sees them. Unfortunately, we live in a culture that has very little value for children. Many consider them a liability and burden, not a blessing. This is why many women are deciding to postpone having children or to skip motherhood altogether.

The "child-free" movement praises women who choose a career over motherhood, treating their choice as a liberation from oppression. Any parent of more than two kids can tell stories of strangers making comments like, "Wow, you've got your hands full," and, "Bless your heart, you must be busy." In America, the majority of us see kids as a burden (at least a little bit), and we can't fathom why anyone would want to have more than one or two. This is very different from God's view of children.

To learn how to contend for our children in prayer, many of us need to first step outside of our cultural beliefs and allow the Spirit to wash our minds and hearts with God's view of children.

The Bible makes it clear our children are immensely valuable. Psalm 127:3-4 gives us one of the most famous biblical statements on children. These verses give us three pictures of the worth of children. They are not a ball and chain, a punishment for sin, or a form of torture. No. Of all the things God could have said about children, He chose these three.

> **Children are gifts.**
> **Children are rewards.**
> **Children are arrows.**

The Gift

When we think of gifts, we tend to think of Christmas or our birthday—the two times of the year when people give us presents. This is the language God uses to describe children. It should not surprise us, since His greatest gift to us was the gift of His Son, our Savior, born into this world as a baby. If God disliked children, He certainly could have come up with another plan of salvation that did not involve becoming a human child. He is brilliantly creative. He could have dreamed up another way. Yet, He didn't. His very best plan meant coming to earth as a baby. It meant being first a child before He became a man.

In this choice, God said something special about children. He first took on flesh as one of the least valued members of first-century culture. In so doing, He said these little ones have great value. Just as Jesus came as a gift to us, so each child that comes into the world is a gift to the world. Each child carries a unique piece of the Father's heart, and each child is destined to bring the Father's love to earth in a unique way. Because of this, every child is a gift and a blessing from Heaven, even before he or she accomplishes anything. This is not just true of some children, but all.

Children are one of life's best gifts.

The word translated in Psalm 127 as "gift" can also be translated as "heritage." This is a word we don't use much today, but it carries an important added meaning. A *heritage* is an inherited possession, or an inheritance. In other words, it implies a legacy or an heirloom that is passed down through the generations. So, when God gives the gift of a child, He gives a piece of His legacy. He is adding to the family inheritance with the wealth of another child from His heart. Every child comes from the Father and is His possession (in the sense that He is the Creator and Sustainer).

Every child is an heirloom in God's family, a valuable treasure that carries the essence of God's royal family line.

All children are gifts to the families they are born into, and they are also gifts to the world as a whole. Think of the incredible value a single person can bring through love, compassion, a heart for justice, a knack for inventing, the wisdom to create systems and structures, artistic skill, and so forth. Each person is a unique and special gift to this world. While we do not all learn how to live up to our potential, and some people bring bad instead of good, the essence of who we are is a good gift from the Father.

We are all created with seeds of greatness and blessing in us because we are all created in our Father's image. Therefore, the worth of a child is not determined by the situation that child is born into or whether adults value him or her. It is determined by the seed of God that resides within.

Understanding this, we can truly look at each child as a gift from God. From His perspective, there's no such thing as an accidental pregnancy or an unwanted child. **All** children originate in His heart and carry His image. **All** children have a gift within them to give to this world. Not just some children. Not just the children born into privilege. Not just the children who have loving parents. It is a great tragedy that many children are born into poverty and hardship. Some are born to parents who do not love them. Some are not even given a chance at life. God does not ordain these situations. It is not His heart that any child should suffer, yet tragically, many do.

The Church has a lot of work to do in helping the children of the world. What we must remember, as we see these children in need, is that their environment and their position do not determine their value. It would not be better if they had not been born. Every child is a gift.

Jesus, more than anyone, understood God's heart for children. In fact, He made some controversial statements about them that undermined the value system of that day. When His disciples began arguing about which of them was the greatest, Jesus called a child to stand before the disciples.

> *Truly I tell you, unless you change and become like little children, you will never enter the kingdom of heaven. Therefore, whoever takes the lowly position of this child is the greatest in the kingdom of heaven.* (Matthew 18:3–4)

Here Jesus holds children up as an example for adults as a gift to show us what Kingdom life looks like. Then, He starts talking about our responsibility toward them.

> *Whoever welcomes one such child in my name welcomes me. If anyone causes one of these little ones—those who believe in me—to stumble, it would be better for them to have a large millstone hung around their neck and to be drowned in the depths of the sea.* (Matthew 18:5–6)

A few verses later, Jesus adds another warning about our view of children: "See that you do not despise one of these little ones. For I tell you that their angels in heaven always see the face of my Father in heaven" (Matthew 18:10). Here, Jesus gives us a further peak into the heart of God toward children. The angels assigned to watch over children have a special and continual access to God the Father. The implication is the angels assigned to adults do not have the same level of direct access. To us, this might seem backwards, but it is a reminder of Heaven's value system, and the place children hold in it.

Powerful Parenting Insights

- Children are **not** burdens, but blessings.
- Children are not just future adults. They have profound value from the very moment they are created.
- In the very core of their nature and personhood, children are a gift.
- **All** children are a heritage from the Lord.
- **All** children belong to Him.
- He gives each child to this world as a gift.

This idea is completely revolutionary in our culture, which values adult choice so highly above the needs of children. But if we, as Christian parents, want to fight for the destinies of our children, we must learn to see them as the gifts they are. We must learn to value them as those who carry a piece of the Father in their hearts and have unique blessings to release upon the earth. Every child—even those who might be called the "trouble child" and the "unwanted child"—is a gift from Heaven.

Pause and Reflect…

How has understanding Heaven's value system adjusted your thinking on fighting for your child's destiny?

The Reward

According to Psalm 127, children are not only a gift, but also a reward. According to the Merriam-Webster Dictionary, the word *reward* means "a thing given in recognition of one's service, effort, or achievement."[3] It conveys appreciation, pleasure, and joy. We could say that a reward is a gift given in appreciation and honor. So, children are not simply an undeserved gift, but they are a reward God gives to us out of His great value for us.

> **God delights in us.**
> **One result of that delight**
> **is the reward of children.**

God's heart toward children is so great, He sees them as a prize. This does not mean we must "earn" the blessing of children through good behavior. The ability to bear children is a reward God has universally given to humanity as a sign of His love for us and His pleasure in us. When people have difficulty conceiving, it is not a curse from God. His will is for everyone to be able to bear children, just as it is His will for everyone to live in health. Thus, we must not see infertility as a lack of blessing, but as a need for healing. God's will is for all married couples to be able to have children.

Not only that, but because God calls children a reward, we can know children are never a sign of God's displeasure or a punishment for sin. By nature, as a reward, they cannot spring from God's disappoint but only from His pleasure. When children are born as a result of sexual sin, it is not God's punishment of the mother and father, but a piece of His redemptive love. The fruit of the womb is always a trophy of God's love, His choice reward. As parents, we should view our children this way. They are a gift and a reward in our lives. This, of course, does not mean that parenting them is always fun and easy.

Powerful Parenting Insights

- ➤ The psalmist doesn't tell us children are a gift and a reward from God because they are always so much fun or they are so sweet and cute.
- ➤ Like the gift of a large house comes with work needed to maintain it, the same is true of children!
- ➤ Yet, the work needed does not negate the fact children are a blessing.
- ➤ Parenting is a challenge, but it is first a reward.

Children have the capacity to bring great joy into our lives. A world without children would be an impoverished one. Their zest, their laughter, their excitement, their innocence, their optimism, their unique way of viewing the world, and more enhance our lives. Yet, children also often present us with tremendous challenges and test our faith and patience beyond what we expect.

Parenting is no small task. It involves its fair share of struggle and trial. It is both an incredible gift and a huge responsibility. This is true not just during the diaper phase or the grade-school phase, but even into adulthood.

Though none of us are truly worthy of such a great gift, God rewards and entrusts us with the care of the children of His heart.

Pause and Reflect…

How has understanding Heaven's reward system adjusted your perspective on parenting your child?

Digging Deeper Workbook Chapters 1-2

Chapters 1-2
God's Value System

Read Psalm 127:3-5.

List the three descriptions in this verse that define God's view of children:

1. _____
2. _____
3. _____

Explain what each of these mean to you as you seek to lead your child toward his or her destiny:

_____
_____
_____
_____
_____

If we want to lead our children toward their destinies, the first step is renewing the way we see them to align with the way God sees them.

Powerful Parenting Insights

- Children are **not** _____, but _____.
- Children have profound _____ from the moment they are created.
- _____ Child is a gift from _____.
- _____ children are a _____ from the Lord.
- _____ children belong to _____.

When God says all or every, what does He mean? _____

Are then any "conditions" or exceptions to what He is saying? _____

Read James 1:5.

Like the gift of a large house comes with work needed to maintain it, the same is true of children! Yet, the work needed does not negate the fact children are a blessing. Parenting is a challenge, but it is first a reward. What challenges have you faced or are facing with your child/children?

_____
_____
_____
_____
_____

Read Jeremiah 29:11.

At the center of God's master plan for transforming the earth into the Kingdom of God is this chain of succession by which fathers and mothers pass along their faith to their children, who then pass it along to their children, and so forth.

If you have not already done so, begin having daily devotions using age-appropriate lessons to include them in the discussions as much as possible. An illustrated children's Bible can prove very helpful.

Review these Powerful Parenting Insights:

➢ Our labor of love in godly parenting should result in seeing both spiritual and natural children walk with God and embrace their destiny in Him.

Are you experiencing this in your natural and spiritual children?

Explain: _____

The path from here to there often is not easy, but if we persevere in faith, love, and prayer, we can see our children walking with the Lord.

Read and Memorize Mathew 19:26.

Pray

Father, I pray _____ would be strengthened and reinforced with mighty power in his/her inner being by the Holy Spirit. May Christ through faith actually dwell (settle down, abide, make His permanent home) in his/her heart! May _____ be rooted deeply in love and founded securely on love, so that he/she may have the power and strength to grasp the experience of that love—what is the breadth and length and height and depth of it. I pray _____ may really come to know practically, through experience for him/herself the love of Christ, which far surpasses mere human knowledge and reasoning. I pray _____ would be filled through all his/her being with all the fullness of God and have the richest measure of Your divine Presence.

Chapter 3
Launching Our Arrows

God sends children into this world as a gift and a reward. This is their nature. As they grow, their destiny is to become like arrows in the Kingdom of God. They are created with a divine purpose, yet they need to grow up into that purpose. Guiding them along this path is one of the main roles God has given parents. It is our great privilege to walk alongside our children and to launch them into their destiny.

The care and guidance parents offer to their children leads to the third aspect of God's value system mentioned in Psalm 127. Children are intended to become like arrows in the hand of a warrior. The psalmist says, "How blessed is the man whose quiver is full of them; they will not be ashamed when they speak with their enemies in the gate" (Psalm 127:5 NASB).

When babies are first born, caring for them is simple. All they need is lots of food, sleep, bathing, and cuddles. However, it's not long before all that changes, and as parents we begin to realize that guiding a child along the right path is not at all easy or simple. Children are a gift and a blessing but raising them right requires a lot of hard work.

One day, we will need to answer to God for how we steward the gifts of the children He gave us. It is important to ask what God requires of us as parents. I believe we find the answer to that in the picture of children as arrows in Psalm 127:4. "Like arrows in the hands of a warrior are children born in one's youth."

The picture painted for us here is of a warrior with arrows in his hand he is ready to shoot at a moment's notice. In the heat of battle, a warrior doesn't have time to make his arrows. He needs to come to the battle prepared with arrows that have already been shaped and sharpened into effective weapons.

We must shape our children into effective arrows. This happens through proper training in life and spiritual matters. Then, we must launch them out into their destinies. One of the best ways we can do this is through effective prayer. In the process of raising children, we are both training and launching them throughout their lives.

Understanding God's Master Plan

At the center of God's master plan for transforming the earth into the Kingdom of God is this chain of succession by which fathers and mothers pass along their faith to their children, who then pass it along to their children, and so forth. No one generation can bring Heaven to earth all on their own.

In His genius, God gave us a simple and remarkable way for the Kingdom to gain momentum from generation to generation. For His plan to work, however, we need to learn to truly disciple our kids, so they do become arrows in His quiver.

Pause and Reflect…

> *How has realizing God's remarkably simple way to transform the earth into the Kingdom of God opened your eyes to the extreme importance of learning to disciple your children?*

> **"I have no greater joy than to hear that
> my children are walking in the truth."**
> **– Apostle John in 3 John 1:4**

John said this of his spiritual children, but the same is true for natural parents. As believers, we are called to parent our natural children and also to spiritually adopt other children and young adults.

Powerful Parenting Insights

- Our children are created with a divine purpose.
- One day, we will need to answer to God for how we steward the gifts of the children He gave us.
- It is important to ask what God requires of us as parents through proper training in life and spiritual matters so we can launch them out into their destinies.
- Fathers and mothers are to pass along their faith to their children, who then pass it along to their children, and so forth.

Embracing the Journey

Now, thirty years later, my kids are grown, and they're embarking on a new phase of life as adults. Yet, the fight for their hearts and destinies continues. It was not always easy to have three little kids all at once. Yet, we had many amazing times together, and I am thankful that even as adults they have remained close to one another and to me.

Many of their friends also became like spiritual children to me (see Isaiah 54:1), and even though they are older now, my heart for them has not changed. It is my great joy and privilege to pray for my own kids and for my spiritual kids. The love God has given me for them is beyond words.

Not long ago, I was reminded, again, of the power of my prayers for the natural and spiritual children God has placed in my life. One of my spiritual kids, who is a friend of my kids and sees me as his God-mom, went through a very rough time after a break-up. Several months before it happened, I had a dream in which I saw him run toward me, sobbing, and he grabbed me and hugged me. I knew in my spirit he and his girlfriend were going to break up, and it would be very hard on him.

Sure enough, three months later my kids told me about it. I felt from God that I should give him some space, so I did for about six months. Then, I texted him and invited him over. While we sat in my backyard, I shared the dream with him.

Then, I looked him in the eyes and said, "I really feel like God gave me that dream because He has someone for you who will love you and be super abundantly above and beyond all you can ask or desire."

Then I added, "But it's really important you don't shut down or close yourself off."

This young man comes from a very emotionally stoic family and tends to be very quiet and emotionally distant. In high school, he was born again, which was a terrific testimony. Yet, even as he got to know Jesus, I had only seen him cry once in the many years I'd known him. In the wake of this heartbreak, I knew he needed to fight the impulse to hide and build walls around his heart because not only would that hurt his relationships with other people, it would especially hurt his relationship with God.

My spiritual son heard me that day, but I could tell his heart was distant.

He shook his head and said, "Okay, God-mom."

I could tell the wounds were deep. I continued to pray and to contend for his destiny, believing God had given me a special role to play because He gave me that dream at such a key time in this young man's life. Sure enough, my spiritual son called me, telling me he has decided he wants to get his life and faith back on track, and he asked me for church recommendations near his university. I am so thankful God has given me a place in this man's life and that I can help birth him into his destiny. What a joy it will be to see what he becomes as he learns to open his heart more and more to his Father in Heaven.

Truly, these children of ours have been sent here to planet earth as a gift from God. His plans for them are incredible, and He has invited us to join with Him in becoming midwives of destiny. It is my prayer that today's generations of children and young adults will truly become a gift and a reward in this world as they are launched like arrows into their destinies by the powerful prayers of their parents.

Digging Deeper Workbook Chapter 3

Read Proverbs 22:6.

How are you going to determine how to parent your child in the way he should go?

Review these Powerful Parenting Insights:

- Our children are created with a _____.
- One day, we will need to answer to God for how we steward the gifts of the children He gave us.
- *What does this mean to you as a parent?*

_____

- *Why is it important to ask what God requires of us as parents through proper training in life and spiritual matters?*

_____

> Fathers and mothers are to pass along their _____ to their children, who then pass it along to their children, and so forth.

Why is this such an important part of your parenting responsibility?

Read and Memorize James 5:16b.

"The prayer of a righteous person is powerful and effective" (NIV).

Pray

I release my faith and declare, Father, that as _____ grows in grace and in the knowledge of our Lord Jesus Christ, he/she will not depart from the faith or from the things he/she has been taught. I pray that every word of God that has been sown into his/her heart will not return void, but will sprout and bring forth abundant fruit in _____'s life. I agree that the Word of God will not depart out of _____'s mouth, but he/she will love Your Word and meditate in it day and night and will observe to do according to all that is written in it. Lord God, I thank You that You will make _____'s way prosperous, and he/she will have good success.

Chapter 4

Training

When we see our children as arrows, we know it is not our job to control our children (and in fact, that it is not even possible to control another person). Instead, it is our job to launch and direct them toward the right goals. We aim them toward the heart of God and trust Him with their futures. As parents, we become their biggest cheerleaders and encouragers, and we create opportunities for them to learn about real-life consequences while they are young so they can grow into great decision-makers.

When we see them as arrows, we train them and use our prayers to aim them toward the straight-and-narrow path. As parents, we can have confidence that our prayers of faith will produce good results in the lives of our children. God's love for them is deep, and He wants them to thrive in life.

Powerful Parenting Insights

- ➢ It is important to remember that God created our children, and they are His more than they are ours.
- ➢ When we train and pray for our kids, our job is not to decide what they should do but to pray that they would find God's best for their lives.
- ➢ We do not always know what's best for them, but God does.

➤ We must train and pray them into their destiny and bless their relationship with God—even if it might look different than what we wanted or expected.

As parents, it is our job from day one to train our children for success in life and in the Kingdom of God. When children are young they are blank slates and are incapable of directing themselves. They rely fully on their parents. As they grow, they gradually become more independent and have more responsibility to direct their own lives. However, the choices they make as they grow stem from the direction they receive when they are little. This is why we must give much attention to guiding our children toward the truth while they are little. Children need direction, and they need boundaries. These serve as a safety net that teaches them how to properly handle themselves in the varied situations they will face in life.

For example, imagine a two-year-old girl who throws herself to the floor and cries if she doesn't get what she wants. If her parents reinforce this behavior by giving her what she wants because she's just so cute, she will learn the way to get what she wants is to be disrespectful. However, if her parents refuse to respond to tantrums and require her to ask kindly before she gets what she wants, she will learn that kindness is more effective. As a two-year-old, she is essentially still a blank slate, absorbing everything from her environment and the people who are closest to her.

The choices parents make when their child is young will affect his or her life as they grow into adulthood.

I believe the reason young children so often disobey and push the boundaries is to see whether their parents really mean what they say. This subconscious need to know their parents are trustworthy is a core part of their development. The knowledge that their parents will follow through and the boundaries are secure is comforting to the psyche of a child. It is like a construction worker who climbs up onto a newly built roof and jumps up and down on it with all his might. He isn't doing this to try to break the roof, but to test it and make sure it is safe and stable.

Children don't realize all this when they disobey. It is a part of their human instinct to search for safety and stability. When we recognize and meet this need, we create an environment in which our children feel secure.[4]

Pause and Reflect...

Do you see why we must give so much attention to guiding our children toward the truth while they are young?

Do you see why children need direction and boundaries?

Are there changes you need to make as you train and guide your child?

None of us walks this out perfectly, yet we can set our children up for success in this if we train and pray for them from a young age to live by God's truth. The wisdom found in Proverbs 22:6 is true: "Start children off on the way they should go, and even when they are old they will not turn from it." Remember that a parent is the first picture of God a child sees.

Anthony

I know a young man named Anthony who was raised in a Christian home. However, as a teen, he began to chase drugs, money, and immoral relationships. During the next fourteen years, his parents prayed earnestly. One night, while they were having a Bible study in their home, Anthony walked in and heard John Bevere talking about those who had strayed so far from God that their hearts were hardened to Him, and he said he feared for their souls. Anthony's parents continued to pray and declared over and over that they would not allow the devil to steal their child's destiny.

Eventually, Anthony's lifestyle caught up with him, and he started having shortness of breath and severe abdominal pain. He ended up collapsing in his apartment, and a friend called 911. After several hours in the emergency room, the doctors diagnosed him with severe congestive heart failure with only 8 percent of his heart was functioning. The doctors told Anthony's parents they didn't think he would survive the night. Anthony's father declared to his wife, "We didn't come this far to give up now. God said our son will live and not die, and he will declare the works of God!"

It was time for war, and that is exactly what Anthony's parents did. They used the doctor's reports as a strategy against the enemy, and they fought in the Spirit for their son's life and salvation.

Anthony did survive the night, and he stayed in the hospital until his heart improved to 15 percent function at which point the doctors sent him home with a pic line pumping medication into his heart. The doctors suggested Anthony get a heart transplant, and they asked the entire family to come to the office to start the process. While the family gathered in the waiting room, the doctor took Anthony back to speak to him alone. Ten minutes later, he came out with tears streaming down his cheeks. "My heart is healed," he said. "I don't need a transplant!"

Anthony's life was forever marked by that experience of God's power and love in his life, and he is still serving God today. Anthony's story is an important reminder. We must not underestimate the power of prayer.

No matter how well (or poorly) we have done training of our children, no matter what circumstances conspire against our children's destinies, we can point them toward their calling in God through prayer.

Pause and Reflect...

How has Anthony's testimony confirmed the truth of Proverbs 22:6?

Determine to continue to train and pray for your children no matter how young or old they are![5]

Digging Deeper Workbook Chapter 4

Read Psalm 90:16.

How are you going to train your children and be an example of God's love and truth for them so they will choose to serve the Lord?

Review these Powerful Parenting Insights:

Powerful Parenting Insights

➤ Why is it so important to remember that God created our children, and they are His more than they are ours?

➤ When we train and pray for our kids, our job is not to decide what they should do but to pray that they would find _____ _____ for their lives.

➤ We do not always know what's best for them, but God does.

➢ We must train and pray them into their destiny and bless their relationship with God—even if it might look different than what we wanted or expected.

List the steps has God revealed to you as you have sought how to train each of your children in keeping with God's purpose for their life:

_____
_____
_____
_____
_____

Read and Declare Isaiah 65:23 Over Each of Your Children Daily

_____ will not labor in vain, nor will _____ be doomed to misfortune; for _____ will be blessed by the LORD, _____ and _____ descendants as well.

Pray

I pray my child _____ and this next generation of young people will become part of a body of believers who are wholly filled and flooded with You! I pray that my child _____ and this generation would rise up and call their parents blessed for training them in the way they should go.

Chapter 5
Prayer

Training and lifting our children up in prayer can help them to develop a healthy relationship with God and with us. They can grow into confident and mature adults who have cultivated the fruit of the Spirit in their lives. In Galatians, the apostle Paul describes the character of a believer.

> *But the fruit of the Spirit is love, joy, peace, patience, kindness, goodness, faithfulness, gentleness, self-control; against such things there is no law. Now those who belong to Christ Jesus have crucified the flesh with its passions and desires. If we live by the Spirit, let us also walk by the Spirit* (Galatians 5:22–25 NASB).

It involves creating a thirst for the spiritual life and directing our children toward faith and life in Christ. It also means giving our children moral guidance and teaching them to obey God, not out of fear but out of love.

**Love is a stronger motivator than fear.
Our God is a God of love.**

God gives us the spirit of adoption into His family, and He takes away the spirit of fear (see Romans 8:15). If we teach our children to obey Him out of fear, that will take them only so far because it misses the essence of the gospel. However, if we teach them to love Him and to obey from love and hunger for His presence, they will be compelled to follow Him because of the connection they have with Him. This is how we effectively fashion arrows that will fly far in the Kingdom.

Our Mistakes Redeemed

This biblical standard for parenting is a high one, and it may be easy to read this and feel like a failure. That is not my goal. No parent is perfect, and most of us make many mistakes along the way. It is a growing experience for both us and our children. Many parents suffer from guilt and shame because they feel like they failed in some way in their parenting. God never wants us to feel shame about the past. He is the redeemer of all things. Remember when you make a mistake, confess, and ask forgiveness. Remember, we may not be perfect parents, but we can be praying parents!

God is the God of restoration and forgiveness.

Pause and Reflect…

> *Take a moment and give your mistakes to God, accept His forgiveness, and allow Him to make something beautiful out of them.*

Praying Effectively

James held up the Old Testament prophet Elijah as an example of an effective prayer warrior, pointing out that "Elijah was a human being, even as we are" (James 5:17). In other words, Elijah had shortcomings and made poor choices, but he had faith in God. It is our faith in Him that makes us righteous, not a perfect past (see Romans 1:17). Thus, along with Elijah, we can be those righteous ones who pray powerful and effective prayers.

> **Remember, "...the prayer of a righteous person is powerful and effective" (James 5:16b).**

Powerful Parenting Insights

- We are not perfect, but we can be powerful prayer warriors for our children.
- Do not accept the enemy's lies when he tells us our mistakes have ruined our children for success.
- Trust God to redeem our mistakes.
- No child is out of God's reach.
- Do not underestimate the power of God's love for our children.

Prayer is one of the most important gifts we can give our children. As their parents, we have spiritual authority in their lives, and we can use that authority for their good. Our children need prayer support at every stage of their lives—while they live at home and after they've become independent adults. When we pray for them, we make them a target for the Holy Spirit. We remove spiritual hindrances and pave a way for God to move powerfully in their lives. Our prayers also establish a spiritual boundary of protection around them. Ezekiel 22:30 talks about our ability to build up the wall or stand in the gap on behalf of others. Through intercession, we create a hedge of physical and spiritual protection around our children.

In Hebrews 4:16, we are told to "come boldly to the throne of grace, that we may obtain mercy and find grace to help in time of need"

(NKJV). To pray boldly means to pray fearlessly and shamelessly. The Greek word used here, *parrhesia*, means "absence of fear in speaking boldly; confidence; cheerful courage."[6] This is how we are invited to pray, not only for ourselves but also for those we love.

God has provided the mercy (forgiveness) and the grace (divine empowerment) that is needed in every situation. No matter how ugly it may look, His mercy and grace are available and more than adequate to help in the situations that concern our children. To access that help, all we need to do is come to Him boldly, in faith, and ask. We don't need to fear or pray prayers born out of fear. We have the Word of God to stand on, and His Word is the final authority in our homes.

Pause and Reflect...

> *How has what you have learned about the power of prayer going to change the way you now pray for your child?*

I will talk in more depth about how exactly we can intercede for our children in another chapter, but for now, the point is our prayers of bold faith have a profound impact on our children's lives. As we learn to be intercessory parents, we will exert remarkable influence over the hearts and destinies of our children. God loves them even more than we do, and He wants them to thrive and succeed. As we pray for our kids, we invite the Creator of the universe to become their champion. He can do so much more for them than we can. He can heal their hearts. He can give them courage, peace, and joy.

God is the one who holds the solutions to the problems they face.

It is important to remember that God created our children, and they are His more than they are ours. When we pray for our kids, our job is not to decide what they should do but to pray that they would find God's best for their lives. We do not always know what's best for them, but God does. This is important. It's easy for us, as parents, to think we know what our kids should do, and it can be tempting to pray from that attitude, but such prayers are soulish and controlling. This is not God's design. Instead, we must pray into their destiny and bless their relationship with God—even if it might look different than what we wanted or expected.

For example, if I wanted one of my kids to become a doctor and prayed and declared along those lines even though the child has shown no interest in being a doctor, that is a soulish and controlling prayer. It is not my job to decide what careers my children should have or to make other major decisions for them. Instead, I should pray God would give them the wisdom to know their calling and that He would open doors and prosper their work.

If, on the other hand, my child is making sinful and harmful decisions, like taking drugs, I need to pray against the influence of the devil, that specific action and declare freedom over my child. Yet, even in doing this, I must leave the door open regarding *how* God wants to work in my child's life.

People often told my daughter Danielle that she should be a doctor, so in her first two years of college, she majored in biology. One day, she called and said she wanted to change her major to Public and Community Service. She didn't want to be a doctor. She is smart and compassionate, and she wanted to help people, but not in the medical field.

As her mom, I was continually declaring the Word of God and praying in tongues over her. I know it was because of my prayers, she responded to her destiny and followed her heart instead of following other people's advice, which in this instance was opposite to her calling. Now, after completing her degree, Danielle went on to Bible school for two years, received training as a ministry leader, then went on to

Boston University, thus completing her master's in theological studies. While in Bible school, Danielle met her husband, and together they are pursuing public ministry as well as community service. My prayers are now for the two of them, that they will continue to grow together and move in their destiny as a couple.

Jeremiah 29:11 encourages us as parents to continually cover our children with our prayers to aim them toward the plan and purpose God has for their lives.

> *"For I know the plans I have for you," declares the* Lord, *"plans to prosper you and not to harm you, plans to give you hope and a future."*

We can have confidence that our prayers of faith will produce good results in the lives of our children. God's deep love for them has destined them for success even before they were born. When you pray Scripture over your child, God's truth is imparted to them through the Teacher of all Truth, the Holy Spirit.

> *Before I formed you in the womb I knew you, before you were born I set you apart; I appointed you as a prophet to the nations.* (Jeremiah 1:5)

Digging Deeper Workbook Chapter 5

Read Romans 1:17.

What did you glean from this scripture about faith and righteousness?

Explain why this is important as you seek to become an effective prayer warrior for your child.

Read Mark 10:27.

Write a testimony of how you have seen this powerful truth proved in your own life, especially in regard to your own child.

Read Jeremiah 1:5.

How has what God said about your child going to help you be an effective prayer warrior for them now and as they move into their calling from God?

Review these Powerful Parenting Insights:

➢ None of us are perfect, but we can be powerful prayer warriors for our children.

Explain how you know this is true:

➢ Do not accept the enemy's lies when he tells you that your mistakes have ruined your children for success.

James 4:7 tells you to _____ yourself to _____; _____ the _____ and he will _____ from you!

➢ Trust God to _____ your mistakes.

How would you explain this to another parent suffering from guilt?

➢ Declare to yourself out loud, "No child is out of God's reach."

➢ Do not underestimate the power of God's love for your children.

Thank Him for His love right now!

Read and Memorize Jeremiah 29:11.

"For I know the plans I have for you," declares the Lord, *"plans to prosper you and not to harm you, plans to give you hope and a future."*[7]

Pray

Father, I pray _____ would be motivated by Your plans and what You have called him/her to be and do. I pray _____ would not lean on his/her own understanding or what society says, but I pray _____ would sense destiny within him/her calling him/her. I speak to the destiny within _____ to come forth in the name of Jesus! I command the blinders to come off of his/her eyes in the name of Jesus. Destiny, arise and come forth! Holy Spirit, Spirit of Truth, please help _____ in this day and hour. Convict and convince _____ of his/her need for Jesus and fill him/her with the desire to serve Jesus as Lord all the days of his/her life.

Chapter 6

The Rising Generations: Millennials

—⋘✦⋙—

Once we have embraced God's view of children and begin to see them as blessings, it is then important to learn to understand the rising generations of young adults, youth, and children and how they differ from previous generations.

Understanding Millennials

The generation of people born between roughly 1980 and 1995 is most often called the Millennial Generation or Generation Y. Other names for Millennials include the Peter Pan Generation and the Boomerang Generation because of this generation's propensity to move back in with their parents, perhaps due to economic constraints, and a growing tendency to delay some of the typical adulthood rites of passage like marriage and starting a career.

Those of us who have children in early adulthood are probably part of the Baby Boomer Generation (born in the 1940s to 1960s) or Generation X, and our kids fall into the Millennial Generation. This means our kids and their peers are approaching life with some very different perspectives from what we grew up with. If we want to bridge that proverbial generation gap, we need to understand the general characteristics of the Millennial Generation and how to best reach them.

Millennial Strengths

Micah Solomon, of *Forbes*, suggests that Millennials possess five key traits as a generation.

1. Millennials value technology.
2. Millennials are a social generation.
3. Millennials collaborate and cooperate.
4. Millennials look for adventure and crave discovery.
5. Millennials are passionate about values.[8]

For many of us in older generations, the way Millennials use technology can seem imbalanced, yet it is actually a strength. In our rapidly changing world, Millennials are comfortable with the tools that will help them stay ahead of the game. They are tech-savvy, which means they're comfortable navigating the rapid changes in the tech world. They embrace change, and they often like being part of creating change. As a whole, Millennials are not prone to being "stuck in their ways" because they grew up adapting to morphing technology. They also grew up with more exposure than previous generations to a variety of cultures and belief systems around the world. This makes them quicker to accept differences in others. Being quick to embrace differences makes them also quick to learn and try new things, which makes them experts at innovation.

Tom Agan, of the *New York Times*, puts it this way: "Social media permeate the personal, academic, political and professional lives of millennials, helping to foster the type of environment where innovation flourishes. So, when compared with older generations, millennials learn quickly—and that's the most important driver of innovation."[9]

Those of us who didn't grow up with social media sometimes feel conflicted about the role of social media in modern life (and not without reason), yet it does have great potential for innovation and impact.

Pause and Reflect...

> *Do you feel conflicted concerning the role of social media in the lives of your children?*
>
> *How has this caused issues in communicating with your children?*

However, the more broadly information is shared, the more innovation flourishes. Millennials love consuming and sharing information online, and this uniquely positions them as a generation to introduce new levels of innovation to "how things have always been done."

As a generation, they place a huge value on transparency, free flow of information, and inclusiveness. The book *Why Nations Fail*, by Daron Acemoglu and James Robinson, talks about the importance of information sharing to innovation and growth on a national level.

Tom Agan applies the same reasoning to the position of Millennials in the workplace, "When a small, closed group of elites holds power, it tends to limit information and education and resist innovations that threaten its strength.... By contrast, innovation thrives when information is unfettered, education is nurtured, people can readily form new groups, and decision-making is inclusive. These circumstances offset the strong tendency of those in power to resist change—in a country or at a company."[10]

The same could be said for the Church. The bottom line is, wherever Millennials go, they offer important perspectives, and the leaders and organizations who embrace them will find themselves catapulted into new levels of creativity and impact.

Mike Marasco, the leader of the NUvention program, says: "Millennials work more closely together, leverage right- and left-brain skills, ask the right questions, learn faster and take risks previous generations resisted. They truly want to change the world and will use technology to do so."[11]

Millennials not only love technology, but they also love collaborating and risk-taking together. For Millennials, the world is a much smaller place, and for the most part, it is exciting, not intimidating, or overwhelming. They want to learn about and from others, and they want to share openly about themselves and their own experiences. Social media and texting have given Millennials access to a much broader pool of relationships, and they are more able to maintain relationships with a larger number of people. Texting, online messaging, and video apps have replaced not only snail mail and email, but even phone calls.

This increase in communication has created a generation desperately hungry to know and be known. They want to travel and discover. As a result of increased travel and access to information, Millennials are also very aware of the injustices of this world, and they are passionate about making a difference. They have the ability to not only learn about but also care deeply about injustices that are not directly affecting them or their own communities. Through social media, they are able to add their voice and their money to the cause.

Millennial Struggles

Every generation faces unique challenges, but not every generation watches the world transform as completely as it has in the last thirty years. The Millennials have stepped into a whole new world compared to the world their parents grew up in. Growing up, I never experienced the pressures my kids and their friends have. It truly was a different world. In part, this is due to technology which can be either a blessing or a curse. Today's young adults were the first to learn to "surf the net" in school. From Instant Messenger and MySpace in the 1990s to Facebook and Twitter in the 2000s, this generation grew up with greater access to people and information than any generation before them. This relational access can be good, but it can also be a heavy burden.

Our country has also rapidly moved into a post-Christian culture, idolization of individuality, subjective morality, and growing confusion about gender and homosexuality. All of this is happening in a cultural environment where divorce, school shootings, human trafficking, and suicide are increasingly common. In the early 1960s, the Supreme Court ruled to remove prayer from schools, and in the years that have followed, we have seen a deepening confusion and immorality infiltrate the schools. Then, at a formative time for Millennials, our nation experienced two significant tragedies that forever marked the Millennial conscience.

On April 20, 1999, the first major school shooting happened at Columbine High School in Littleton, Colorado. Two angry students gunned down twelve of their peers and one teacher before taking their own lives. Suddenly, school was no longer a safe place. Many schools have enhanced their security and installed metal detectors. Students no longer experience only earthquake and fire drills, but also active shooter drills. This, I believe, created an expectation, especially among Christian Millennials, that they may become martyrs, like Cassie of Columbine.

Two years later, on September 11, 2001, as the Millennials were between infancy and college age, a new level of fear and instability was introduced to our national psyche when terrorists hijacked four airplanes and flew them into the twin towers in New York City and the

U.S. Pentagon. Not only was this the largest attack on U.S. soil, but it also introduced terrorism to the national conscience.

The combined effect of these two events on Millennials should not be overlooked. In the years when Millennials were developing their self-concept and expectations of the world, generalized fear and instability were normalized.

Alissa Wilkinson, a Millennial herself, puts it this way: "Columbine was also a watershed moment in the consciousness of American teenagers—a moment where safety started to feel like an illusion, and you could be exposed to danger anywhere: at home, at the grocery store, at the mall, in the classroom. That generation would live through the events of 9/11 just two years later, and those two moments define the world for older American millennials, who live in the shadow of acts of large-scale, senseless violence that render even home soil unsafe."[12]

I will never forget where I was on Tuesday, September 11, 2001, when I heard about the attacks of the Muslim terrorist group, al-Qaeda, against the United States. Not only did 9-11 change our country, but it changed me.

At that time, I was preparing to move our family to a new home in another town, and as part of the transition, the school system had allowed my children to begin attending school in their new district even though we had not yet closed on our new home. That morning, I drove my kids to their new school, and on my way home, I heard on the radio that an American Airlines airplane had just crashed into one of the twin towers of the World Trade Center complex in New York City. Shortly after, the radio announcer said another airplane had crashed into the other tower. I knew something was very wrong, and I was terrified.

As I listened to the news reports of these almost incomprehensible events, I felt compelled to pick my children up from school. In the midst of such terror, I needed them by my side. I needed to know they were safe. When I got there, many other mothers were also picking up their children. We were all shaken beyond what we could explain, and at the root of that was an instinctive fear for our children. How do we raise them in a world like this? How do we keep them safe and prepare them for the future?

When I told my kids what had happened, one of them said, "Mommy, I thought you said this would never happen in our nation."

How could I respond to that? It shook me to not be able to reassure my children that everything would be okay. All I could say was, "Well, Mommy was wrong." A new normal had been introduced.

Pause and Reflect…

> *Think about where you and your children were on the morning of 9/11.*
>
> *What were you feeling?*
>
> *How did you explain to your children what was going on?*

Contending for Your Children

> *But this is what the LORD SAYS: "YES, CAPTIVES WILL BE TAKEN FROM WARRIORS, and plunder retrieved from the fierce; **I will contend with those who contend with you, and your children I will save.**"* (Isaiah 49:25 emphasis added)

Two weeks later, I had a speaking engagement. It was the first time God spoke to me about contending for our children.

I had taken a break from ministry after having kids and this was one of the first speaking engagements I'd had in years. To me, it seemed like no mistake that God had opened this door for me and given me this message in the wake of this great disaster in our nation. I found that everyone at the meeting—moms and dads alike—was in shock. The question pulsing through the room was, *What about our kids?* I felt it in my spirit, and the Holy Spirit within me responded.

For the first time ever, I felt like God literally spoke through my mouth about our children and their calling. Before I knew what was happening, I was declaring, "They were born for a time such as this! God equips those He calls, and there is something on the inside of these kids that is unlike anything that previous generations have carried. They are equipped to live in these times!"

Powerful Parenting Insights

- ➤ **God will work with us as we contend [fight] for our children.**
- ➤ **Contending for our children includes understanding God has equipped our children for such a time as this.**
- ➤ **Contending also includes cooperating with their individual God-given calling.**

Such a Time as This

Millennials grew up with stories of large-scale, senseless violence happening at random times and in random places, as people were going about their normal lives. The belief that something terrible could happen at any moment when one least expects it, has created a deep-seated sense of insecurity and instability. On top of that, in 2000 and 2008 our nation experienced two economic crashes. Even if one managed to stay alive, the quality of life was now uncertain.

As Alex Williams, of the *New York Times*, puts it: "Millennials, after all, were raised during the boom times and relative peace of the 1990s, only to see their sunny world dashed by the Sept. 11 attacks and two economic crashes, in 2000 and 2008. Theirs is a story of innocence lost."[13]

Many have described Millennials as being entitled and narcissistic. This rises from the belief they are lazy and prone to jump from job to job. In 2008, Ron Alsop wrote a book about Millennials titled *The Trophy Kids Grow Up*.[14] He suggests that because many Millennials were rewarded in childhood for minimal accomplishments (such as participation) in competitive sports, they have unrealistic expectations of working life. Along these same lines, according to a story in *Time* magazine, recent polls show that Millennials "want flexible work schedules, more 'me time' on the job, and nearly nonstop feedback and career advice from managers."[15]

An even harsher commentary appeared in a *Time* article titled, *Millennials: The Next Greatest Generation?* "They're narcissistic. They're lazy. They're coddled. They're even a bit delusional. Those aren't just unfounded negative stereotypes about 80 million Americans born roughly between 1980 and 2000. They're backed up by a decade of sociological research."[16]

Yet, if we look at these stereotypes without considering the bigger picture, we risk missing an important part of what makes Millennials tick. The organization Project Time Off has suggested, based on their research about employee vacations, that what looks like entitlement in many Millennials is actually fear. In fact, "compared to Boomers, Millennials are at least twice as likely to say there are fearful of losing their job."[17] They worry constantly about what the boss thinks, and they fear being seen as replaceable.

This is a result, at least in part, that Millennials began entering the workforce during an economic downturn. Many of them searched long and hard before they were able to land a job, therefore, they are very ambitious and want to prove their competence in the workplace. As a result, they are less likely to use their vacation days, and even when they do, they often still work online.

According to Project Time Off: "Millennials are also the first generation to experience internet and email as a fixture of their work-life from day one. These digital natives view and use technology differently than older generations. They are more likely to stay plugged in, and less likely to benefit from time off."[18]

This paints a different picture that gives us an important clue to what drives the Millennial psyche. Many of them feel like their environment is insecure and unstable. They crave approval and applause, not because they're self-obsessed, but because they want assurance they're not replaceable. When they're clingy and demanding, it's because they are testing the waters and looking for certainty and security. If they hesitate about big career and life decisions, it's because—while they are hopeful—they are also aware they live in an ever-shifting economic landscape, and they want to make the best decision they can.

In looking at the strengths and struggles of Millennials, it may seem like we have looked at two different groups of people. Millennials are passionate about technology and collaboration. They crave relationships that are real and transparent; they long to be known. They also hunger for adventure and fight for justice. All this is true, and it is balanced atop the sometimes subconscious fear and insecurity rooted in the instability of their growing-up years.

**The good news is,
God created Millennials with an amazing set of traits,
and He wants to free them from their fear
so they can run boldly into their future.**

**He also wants to equip them to lead
the generations that will follow, starting with Generation Z.**

Digging Deeper Workbook Chapter 6

Read Isaiah 49:25.

> *But this is what the Lord says: "Yes, captives will be taken from warriors, and plunder retrieved from the fierce; I will contend with those who contend with you, and your children I will save."*

Define the word "contend":

What does this mean to you as you pray for our rising generations?

Review these Powerful Parenting Insights:

Powerful Parenting Insights

- ➢ **God will work with us as we contend [fight] for our children.**
- ➢ **Contending for our children includes understanding God has equipped our children for such a time as this.**
- ➢ **Contending also includes cooperating with their individual God-given calling.**

List the ways you have observed God has equipped each of your children for such a time as this:

What have you discovered is each of your children's God-given calling?

Read and Memorize 2 Peter 3:9.

The Lord is not slow in keeping his promise…He is patient with you, not wanting anyone to perish.

Pray

Father, I see an army of young men and women rising in this hour. Soldiers—men and women who are armed and dangerous to the kingdom of darkness. May You anoint them with fresh oil more than any other generation. You said in Your Word that where sin abounds Your grace abounds so much more, so I ask for an abundance of grace, an abundance of signs and wonders and miracles to be manifest to this generation. As a natural/spiritual parent, I agree with Your will that not one of them would be lost, but all of them would be saved and come to the knowledge of the truth.

But where sin abounded, grace abounded much more.
(Romans 5:20 NKJV)

Write a specific declaration as you contend for each of your children:

Chapter 7

The Rising Generations: Generation Z

Two weeks after September 11, 2001, I had declared to concerned parents, "They [our children] were born for a time such as this! God equips those He calls, and there is something on the inside of these kids that is unlike anything that previous generations have carried. They are equipped to live in these times!"

This promise has held me during difficult times with my own kids, and I have fallen in love with the rising generations and the special gifts they carry. Mental health experts may be uncertain about how to help Millennials and Generation Z deal with their anxiety and confusion, but we have the answer in Jesus. God is the ultimate expert at delivering people from darkness and bringing them into His marvelous light (see 1 Peter 2:9).

Powerful Parenting Insights

- ➤ In Him, we have the answer our kids need.
- ➤ In Him, we have the solutions to the struggles our children face.
- ➤ In Him, our children can find the security, identity, and confidence they need to thrive in any situation.

Understanding Generation Z

Generation Z, the generation following the Millennials (or Generation Y), is comprised of today's teens and grade school children, those born roughly between 1996 and 2011.

Gen Z Strengths

Tim Elmore runs an international non-profit organization called Growing Leaders, which focuses on mentoring upcoming leaders. His primary focus is on leaders within the Millennials and Generation Z. On his blog, Elmore lists six characteristics he has observed as he has worked with emerging Gen Z leaders.

1. **Cynical** – Compared to Millennials, "They tend to be more realistic not idealistic, seemingly jaded from the tough economy, terrorism and complexities of life."
2. **Private** - They watched the Millennials get in trouble through over-posting and being too transparent online. The world of terrorists and predators is normal, and safety is a major concern. Therefore, Generation Z is much more likely to use private social media sites like SnapChat and Whisper, rather than Facebook.
3. **Entrepreneurial** - Growing up with access to large amounts of information, they are naturally innovative. They don't want to just plug into a day job. They want to pioneer. They're surrounded with stories of internet successes, even teens whose YouTube channels have gone viral. To Generation Z, the world is full of opportunity, yet they're cynical, so they know it'll take hard work. They've taken the innovative spirit of the Millennials and married it with pragmatism, caution, and sensibility.

4. **Multi-tasking** - The increase in technology has only increased the demand for multi-tasking, and today's children and teens are pros at it even before they have had their first job. While Millennials generally prefer two screens, recent studies show Gen Z prefers five screens at once. They are taking multi-tasking to a whole new level. However, although they can get a lot done at once, they are also easily distracted.
5. **Hyper-aware** - "Because their minds are streaming in so many directions, they've become post-moderns who are hyperaware of their surroundings." They have learned from a young age to always be observing life and people through multiple venues. Many of them don't know how to sit and have a conversation with another person without also checking in with the online world on their phone at the same time. Generation Z is hardly ever "off the grid."
6. **Technology-reliant** - Millennials are addicted to their smartphones, but Generation Z is taking that addiction to a new level. They have never lived without technology at their fingertips, and they cannot imagine doing without it. The online world is sometimes more real to them than the people and places in front of them. Because of this, they often find face-to-face relationships challenging.[19]

According to Elmore, this is the shape of the future. Generation Z is deeply immersed in technology, yet they crave structure, stability, and safety. Lucie Greene, the worldwide director of the Innovation Group at J. Walter Thompson, says, Generation Z is "conscientious, hard-working, somewhat anxious and mindful of the future."[20] They have replaced Millennial optimism with cynicism and pragmatism, yet they are hard-working and innovative.

In this, Theo Priestley, a contributor to *Forbes*, finds great hope. He predicts Generation Z will be known as the Builder Generation—as "ones who will build on the foundation that the Millennial generation has sought to put in place through disruption."[21] Priestley continues, "This is a maker generation, a far more pragmatic and practical generation who must architect and build the future we are all trying to imagine living in. The world doesn't need more foundational layers, it needs a generation to create.[22]

Gen Z Struggles

If Millennials were inundated with post-Christian culture, individuality, and subjective "truth," Generation Z has faced these pressures on an even greater scale. In American culture at large, Christians have been labeled as hateful bigots, and it is harder than ever to stand up for Christian morality.

It is no longer culturally acceptable to say one does not affirm the gay lifestyle. Morphing ideas about gender have caused many children and young adults to struggle to find their identities. The cultural focus on LGBTQ+ rights has escalated, and transgender individuals are being portrayed as cultural heroes. Some parents are even using hormones to stunt the natural process of puberty in their children because they believe their children "identify" as a different gender than their biological parts. Trying to navigate these questions while also going through the tumult of puberty has created increased levels of anxiety in Generation Z.

For many of today's teens, their lives online are just as real, if not more real, than the people and places in front of them. This can easily widen the parent-child gap, as children are drawn deeper into their online world and become more isolated from their parents, who "just don't get it."

In her book, *Switch on Your Brain*, communication pathologist and audiologist Dr. Caroline Leaf talks about the importance of limiting screen time, especially when it is what she calls "multitasking media."

Much of technology and social media encourages us to jump from idea to idea rapidly—to multitask—without deep thought. She argues this is the opposite of how our brains are designed to work, and it can cause a level of brain damage often incorrectly diagnosed as ADD or ADHD. "Our brain," she says, "responds with healthy patterns, circuits, and neurochemicals when we think deeply, but not when we skim only the surface of multiple pieces of information."[23]

Even one generation ago, kids spent a significant amount of time playing outdoors and reading books. Now, instead of these focused activities, many kids spend their time being entertained by devices. In fact, scientists have found that the amount of time the average American young person spends multitasking has increased by 120 percent in the last fifteen years. On average, today's teens are exposed to eight and a half hours of multitasking electronic media per day.[24]

Research shows that multitasking social media can be as addictive as drugs and alcohol. If children are developing this addiction before they even hit puberty, it has the potential to have a powerful and detrimental impact on their lives. The impact of multitasking media in childhood and the teen years is significant because it interferes with normal child and adolescent brain development.

According to Dr. Leaf, "Multitasking decreases our attention, making us increasingly less able to focus our thought habits. This opens us up to shallow and weak judgments and decisions and results in passive mindlessness."[25]

Not only that, but it also increases stress. A report in the *Archives of General Psychiatry* shows a connection between simultaneous exposure to electronic media (using multiple devices at once) during the teen years and increased anxiety and depression in young adulthood.[26] When it comes to social media in particular, though many people feel driven to increase their number of friends, studies show that the more social circles a person is linked to, the more likely it is that social media will be a source of stress for that person.[27] Though they crave it, because their brains are addicted to the constant notifications, it also causes anxiety. Not only are they never able to unplug from friend drama and pressures, but their brains are not able to get the quiet time they need for deep thinking. Though their still-developing brains need downtime to create emotional stability, many of them never truly rest their minds.

According to a study performed at the University of Washington, those who practice quieting their minds and deep thinking: "had fewer negative emotions, could stay on task longer, had improved concentration, switched between tasks more effectively in a focused and organized way…and spent their time more efficiently."[28]

Unfortunately, many in Generation Z have no idea how to do this, because they are growing up surrounded by electronic devices and social media. They are always being stimulated by screens, and they cannot escape relational drama online. Cell phones literally allow many kids to socialize at every hour of the day (and night), and on average, according to a Pew study, they send and receive 88 texts per day. In other words, as Joel Stein at *Time* puts it, "They're living under the constant influence of their friends."[29]

When we combine the questions about identity, the lack of a moral compass, and the effects on the brain of digital multitasking with the increased social pressure teens experience online, it is not surprising that many of Generation Z's children and teens are struggling emotionally. In a recent *Times* article, Susanna Scrobsdorff notes the overwhelming emotional pressure that many pre-teens and teens feel in the age of constant access to the Internet. More than in previous generations, today's teens are anxious, depressed, and overwhelmed. This is true not only of kids who come from abusive and troubled homes, but also of those who come from prosperous and happy families. Their stress springs not from their environment as much as the toll of continual multitasking and communication online. As a result, a rising number are engaging in self-harm and even committing suicide, and experts are struggling to know how to help them.[30]

The Help They Need

Both Millennials and Generation Z have amazing qualities and strengths, as well as deep areas of fear and insecurity. The good news is, as their parents, it is our job to both believe in them and to help them overcome their struggles. It is often true our greatest hurdle can become our greatest strength. I believe when our kids learn to overcome their fears and addictions, they will be empowered to help their peers in a powerful way, and they will have the potential to change the world for good.

Powerful Parenting Insights

- ➤ The truth is, it all begins with us!
- ➤ Though we may feel incapable, the truth is we are not.
- ➤ God has given us what we need to succeed.

Digging Deeper Workbook Chapter 7

Read 1 Peter 2:4-5, 9.

> *Coming to Him as to a living stone, rejected indeed by men, but chosen by God and precious, you also, as living stones, are being built up a spiritual house, a holy priesthood, to offer up spiritual sacrifices acceptable to God through Jesus Christ.*
>
> *But you are a chosen generation, a royal priesthood, a holy nation, His own special people, that you may proclaim the praises of Him who called you out of darkness into His marvelous light.*

Write out your declarations over your children based on these powerful descriptions of them from God's Word.

Read Joel 2:28.

> *I will pour out my Spirit on all people. Your sons and daughters will prophesy, your old men will dream dreams, your young men will see visions.*

Review these Powerful Parenting Insights:

Powerful Parenting Insights

- ➤ In Him, we have the answer our kids need.
- ➤ In Him, we have the solutions to the struggles our children face.
- ➤ In Him, our children can find the security, identity, and confidence they need to thrive in any situation.

Powerful Parenting Insights

- ➤ The truth is, it all begins with us!
- ➤ Though we may feel incapable, the truth is
- ➤ God has given us what we need to succeed.

Read and Memorize the words of Jesus in John 14:12

> *"Most assuredly, I say to you, he who believes in Me, the works that I do he will do also; and greater works than these he will do, because I go to My Father."*

Pray

I declare that our youth have strength for all things in Christ, who empowers them. They are ready for anything and equal to any task because Christ infuses them with His strength on the inside. They are self-sufficient in Christ's sufficiency. They will do above and beyond all we can ask or imagine—performing greater works than Jesus did for the glory of God!

Pause and Reflect...

> *How has understanding more about what Generation Z children are facing helped you contend and pray more targeted prayers for your children?*

Chapter 8

The Elisha Company (Part 1)

God's plan for this generation is to bring them into their Promised Land where they can thrive and live out their callings. Yet, like the Israelites of old, they may face many hurdles along the way. As their parents (both in the natural and the spirit), we are capable guides. God has given us His Spirit to help us know how to lead them toward the truth. We are equipped to parent our children with the wisdom of God, the Word of God, and the Spirit of God.

Powerful Parenting Insights

- ➢ We must understand the challenges and pressures our children face, like the men of Issachar "who understood the times and knew what Israel should do." (1 Chronicles 12:32)
- ➢ We must remember that no matter what giants they may face, God is faithful and loving, and He is able to do exceedingly and abundantly above and beyond all we could ask or dream (see Ephesians 3:20). As Steve Backlund often says, "Every area of our life not glistening with hope is under the influence of a lie."[31]
- ➢ They are an Elisha generation who will do twice as much for the Kingdom as the generations before them.

Marked by God

Today's young adults, youth, and children are specially marked by God and specifically chosen to live in this time in history. Before we were even born, God not only knew us, but He destined us for particular good works during our lives on earth (see Ephesians 2:10). Every individual has a unique call, and on a larger scale, every generation has a unique call.

God has appointed us for a particular time in history, and He has equipped us to live and thrive in it. He puts within us what we need to expand the Kingdom in the era we live in.

**No matter what they face,
God has built within our kids the characteristics they need
to overcome and to be victorious in this time in history.**

In the first century, believers faced great peril, but they also had the uniquely special privilege of being the first generation of Christians. They were the first generation to experience the new covenant and declare it to the world. They literally turned their world upside down! God had uniquely chosen and prepared them. Every generation since the first century has also had a unique calling and has also been uniquely equipped to fulfill that calling in a particular era.

If we want to launch our children into their destinies, we need to see that their generation is special and amazing, and they have a unique call from God.

The onus is on us to disciple, to encourage, and to promote as spiritual leaders and prophetic watchmen who have what it takes to launch these next generations into their calling. This is true of all parents.

As their mothers and fathers, we are not called to be afraid, but to intercede for our children. They need our prayers because the enemy wants to stop our children. Our children are depending on us. They are marked by God, but they need our help.

It is not the season to grow weary or lose heart. Instead, we must take the words of Isaiah to heart and rise up in hope: "Those who hope in the Lord will renew their strength. They will soar on wings like eagles; they will run and not grow weary, they will walk and not be faint" (Isaiah 40:31).

Powerful Parenting Insights

- We must rise up like Deborah, who stepped up as a mother, a leader, and a prophet when her people were in need.
- We must take our place as watchmen in our own homes.
- We must stand in faith and hope.
- We must declare over our children they will prophesy, dream dreams, and walk in greater levels of the fruits and gifts of the Spirit. They will fulfill their destinies.
- They will be anointed with fresh oil, and they will carry the torch of revival to the world.

Their Spiritual DNA

Though we won't read about it in secular magazines, the Millennial Generation and Generation Z are marked with certain characteristics, or spiritual DNA, preparing them to live in this era and to advance the Kingdom of God. The first two characteristics are signs and wonders and a boldness to share the love of God.

Signs and Wonders

Millennials and Gen Z-ers are uniquely positioned to walk in greater levels of signs and wonders. In Dutch Sheets' word for 2017, he prophesied we will see an Elisha company of young people who have a double portion of the anointing.[32] Just as Elisha received a double portion of Elijah's anointing when he watched Elijah ascend to Heaven in a whirlwind, so too the whirlwind of the Holy Spirit will bring this double portion of the anointing upon these young people.

It has been more than 100 years since the Azusa Street revival shook the world with the advent of the Pentecostal movement. In the early years, many amazing things happened, yet there was also much error and even spiritual abuse. Today's young adults have learned from the mistakes of previous generations and are starting out in their spiritual journeys with significantly more exposure, teaching, training, and understanding about the things of the Spirit than any generation before them.

As parents and leaders in their lives, we must encourage our children's search and support their desire for training. Though many youth and young adults are leaving traditional churches, they are very hungry for authentic spiritual experiences. This is exactly what we can offer them.

As a leader, I am very conscious of the leading of the Spirit when it comes to imparting spiritual knowledge and laying hands on the members of the younger generations. When I was just 20 years old and graduating from Rhema Bible College, Kenneth E. Hagin interrupted the planned events and said he felt impressed to have an older, more experience married couple, who were also pastors, come to the front and pray for the graduates. This couple had a very spiritually mature church that operated in the gifts of the Spirit and spiritual discernment. Hagin asked this couple to stretch their hands toward the Bible school students and said he believed the wisdom and maturity in the Spirit they had learned over forty years would be transferred from them to the students.

I didn't feel anything when they prayed, but it wasn't long before I began to notice I had a greater intuition about how to walk in the

Spirit and flow prophetically. I began to walk in those realities because of that impartation.

I believe I have the ability and responsibility to impart what I have received spiritually to younger believers. I know God has powerful things in store for Millennials and Generation Z-ers because He has positioned them to walk in greater levels of anointing than previous generations. When one generation learns to walk in the Spirit, and then members of that generation spiritually impart what they have received to younger generations, the anointing is transferred exponentially.

This transferal happens through the company we keep, through the laying on of hands as mentioned in Paul's letters to his spiritual son, Timothy, and through discipleship or closely following a particular leader. Through this sort of impartation, today's young adults, teens, and even children are beginning to walk in greater levels of power and understanding because they are building upon the experience of several generations of believers who have operated in these gifts.

Pause and Reflect…

> *Think about the spiritual training you received as you grew and moved into adulthood. Have you begun to share what you learned with your children?*

Boldness

The upside of our culture's increasing focus on individuality is that it has helped to birth a generation of Christian youth and young adults who are becoming secure in their identity in God and are not afraid of being different. Past generations put a much greater emphasis on conformity. Though peer pressure certainly still exists, today the idea of "being different" has empowered many young people to stand up boldly for their faith and to fully be themselves, no matter what anyone thinks. This makes them great pioneers of the faith who are not held back by fear of others. They love God passionately, and they are compelled to share that love with the world.

In Numbers 14:24, God says that Caleb stood out from his peers because his heart belonged fully to God. Because of this boldness and single focus that could not be swayed by the opinions of others, Caleb was one of the few people from his generation who lived to see the Promised Land. I believe today's rising generations are like Caleb. They are bold and wholeheartedly committed to God, and because of that, they will see great fruit and learn to walk in their destinies. God will "bring them into the land" just like He did for Caleb.

Christian Millennials are passionate about sharing the gospel and impacting culture with God's love. This is important because their own generation is becoming increasingly unchurched. According to Pew research, one-fourth of Millennials are completely unaffiliated with any religion.[33] The world and the rising generations need a real encounter with the love of God. The rising generation of Millennial leaders carries a passion to change their world for God. They are not content to simply sit in a pew one day a week. They want to actually see the Kingdom spread and impact their own culture and the world.[34]

Digging Deeper Workbook Chapter 8

Read **1 Timothy 4:14.**

What does this verse instruct us to do and then train our children to do?

How are you implementing this in your life?

Read **2 Timothy 1:5-14.**

Verse 5 explains Timothy's sincere faith came from:

Verse 6 reminds Timothy to:

Verse 7 encourages Timothy saying:

Verses 8-14 give Paul's spiritual son encouragement to:

Read Psalm 78:1–4.

> *My people, hear my teaching; listen to the words of my mouth. I will open my mouth with a parable; I will utter hidden things, things from of old— things we have heard and known, things our ancestors have told us. We will not hide them from their descendants; we will tell the next generation the praiseworthy deeds of the* LORD, *his power, and the wonders he has done.*

List the ways this passage tells us we are to help prepare our children for such a time as this:

Review these Powerful Parenting Insights:

Powerful Parenting Insights

> ➢ We must understand the challenges and pressures our children face, like the men of Issachar "who understood the times and knew what Israel should do." (1 Chronicles 12:32)

List the challenges and pressures you see your children facing.

Pray and seek God for each one and how to help your children understand the times and know what they should do.

Record what God reveals to you.

> ➢ We must remember that no matter what giants they may face, God is faithful and loving, and He is able to do exceedingly and abundantly above and beyond all we could ask or dream (see Ephesians 3:20). As Steve Backlund often says, "Every area of our life not glistening with hope is under the influence of a lie."[35]

Prayerfully consider an area in your life that is not glistening with hope. What lie is influencing this area of your life?

How is it affecting your children's ability to fulfill their call from God?

> ➢ They are an Elisha generation who will do twice as much for the Kingdom as the generations before them. This means they need twice as much prayer, training, and mentoring.

Begin to double your prayer life, as well as the training and mentoring of your children using the next set of Powerful Parenting Insights.

Powerful Parenting Insights

> ➢ We must rise up like Deborah, who stepped up as a mother, a leader, and a prophet when her people were in need.
> ➢ We must take our place as watchmen in our own homes.
> ➢ We must stand in faith and hope.

➢ We must declare over our children they will prophesy, dream dreams, and walk in greater levels of the fruits and gifts of the Spirit. They will fulfill their destinies.
➢ They will be anointed with fresh oil, and they will carry the torch of revival to the world.

Read and Memorize Isaiah 40:31.

"Those who hope in the Lord will renew their strength. They will soar on wings like eagles; they will run and not grow weary, they will walk and not be faint."

Pray

I pray our children and youth will be a generation who, like the first-century believers, turns the world upside down with the gospel and the flames of a revival spirit. May the river of God rise up from within them, like an artesian well, so much that they won't be able to contain the river arising in their hearts. I pray that from this river would come a greater measure of boldness, that they would open their mouths boldly and make known the mystery of the gospel to their generation. I break the spirit of fear and intimidation that would keep them from announcing their faith to their peers in Jesus' name.

Chapter 9
The Elisha Company (Part 2)

Authenticity

The rising generations place a huge value on authenticity. They have no interest in a polished, fake church, where everyone acts as though their lives are perfectly amazing all the time. They want a real experience with people who own up to their shortcomings and struggles. As those who were raised during the advent of the internet and social media, Millennials and Gen Z-ers find beauty in who people really are, mess and all. According to Karl Moore, at *Forbes*, "Postmoderns want to be able to be themselves. They are not interested in playing 'the game' their parents once did."[36]

A recent article in *The Washington Times*, titled "Millennials Prefer the Real Deal," talks about what it looks like, practically, to be authentic. In summary, the article said to be authentic one must do a better job of communicating (social media), being transparent (show what happens behind the scenes), being relevant (align with millennial wants and needs), and care (show that you provide something of value to the world).[37]

Authenticity involves caring about the world. Our Millennials and Gen Z-ers want to meet people where they are. They are mission-driven, not self-serving. They lead with their hearts, not just their minds, and they consider the long-term impact of their decisions upon others. Authentic leaders are self-aware enough to acknowledge their imperfections and mistakes, recognize what they're good at, and also where they fall short. They are also quick to pull on people who are strong where they are weak and to delegate to their team. They are not a one-person show.

Commonality

Today's youth and young adults value commonality. In other words, they do not look to the person on the stage as "the man of God" or "the woman of God." They believe we all carry the anointing and are all called to do the work of ministry. It's not about being a super-star minister but about spreading the gospel and loving people, whether they are called to a position of leadership in the Church or not. These generations believe the five-fold ministers named in Ephesians 4 are not called to do all the ministry but to **train all believers** to do the ministry.

This mindset shift is summed up well in the phrase coined by some Christian Millennials, who believed themselves called to be a "nameless, faceless generation." Worship leader Jason Upton used it as a sort of battle cry in his song "Lion of Judah":

> There's a new generation arising
> A nameless, faceless, placeless tribe
> All they fear is the fear of the Lord
> All they hear is the Lion of Judah[38]

By nameless and faceless, Upton and others didn't mean unknown or unimportant to God. Today's young people believe we can all walk in great anointing like Benny Hinn or Kathryn Kuhlman. While they honor these great leaders, they do not believe they are set apart or unique. Instead, we are all a royal priesthood. We can all access by faith the same level of breakthrough and even greater because we all have the same Spirit living within us.

To Millennials and Gen Z-ers, it's not about the personality upfront. It's about the Spirit moving. It is about the Spirit empowering a whole generation to walk in step with Him to birth the revival the Church is longing for. It's all about teamwork, sharing the load, and working together.

> **The younger generations realize no one individual can get the job done. We all need to rise up together if we want to truly impact our world.**

Community

The fruit of authenticity and commonality is family. When people are real about their struggles and process, and when they value working together and believe we all play an important part, the result is a sense of belonging and safety. They don't want to just clock in at church on Sunday morning and then go about their normal lives the rest of the week. They want their church community to be an intimate part of their lives. They want the church to look less like a corporation and more like a loving family. They want this family to be multicultural.

Today's young adults and teens grew up with the world at their fingertips, and the differences between people that seemed so large to previous generations are much less intimidating to these younger generations. Instead, they passionately embrace the world in all its beautiful variety and try to make the "foreign" into a family.

The rising generations spend a lot of time on social media, and they have a deep hunger for real connection with others. Their appetite for a family has been whetted by social media, but it cannot satisfy their craving. This is a wide-open door for the gospel if it comes in the form of community and family. Many Millennial leaders are recognizing this need and working to make their expression of the church more relational. After all, the Kingdom of God is all about restoring the relationship between a loving Father and His lost kids.

Truly the Millennial Generation and Generation Z have an incredible call and anointing. I believe God has knit these passions into the hearts of these generations because it is exactly what the Church and the world need.

God of the Impossible

We may look at our children and think, *How is this possible?* This may be especially true if our children are not walking with God. No matter what behaviors they are manifesting right now, they are called by God to be amazing in His Kingdom. They have His gold hidden in their hearts.

Often, when our kids go through hard times or walk away from God, it is because the enemy fears them, and he is working overtime to take them away from their calling. He has been around long enough to recognize the gifts that often accompany certain personalities and temperaments, and he tries to target these children and teens during the vulnerable years when they are discovering who they are. He lies to them and tells them they are nothing because he is terrified of what they could become. He is afraid that they will tap into all God has created them to be and that they will rise up to be a generation of giant slayers. That is why he works so hard to get into their minds and lead them astray.

Pause and Reflect…

> When we see our kids struggling or under attack, we must ask ourselves what it is about our kids that is so terrifying to the enemy?

What call or gift is making the enemy tremble?

We must learn to discern our children's calling, as well as their personalities and unique needs. Different people need different things to thrive in life, and when we know that about our children, we can help them learn how to overcome. When we believe our kids are called by God, we can counter the voice of the enemy by continually speaking to their destiny and telling them they are amazing.

Powerful Parenting Insights

- **One of our main assignments as parents is to be spiritual shields for our children so they can walk through the enemy's attacks unharmed.**
- **We do this with our words, our love, and through prayer.**

When my kids were in junior high, I met a woman who was the mother of a friend of my kids who attended public school with them. She and I started going on regular walks together and the subject of God would often come up. Eventually, I found the courage to ask her if she'd ever heard of the baptism of the Spirit. She said she hadn't, but that she wanted it. So that day we went back to my house, and after telling her all about the baptism of the Spirit, I prayed with her to receive it. When we prayed, she was radically born again and filled with the Spirit. It was incredible!

I felt I needed to disciple her in her faith and teach her how to pray, so we began meeting once a week to pray together. I thought we'd pray for the world and the United States, but instead, we always seemed to end up praying for our kids. Week after week, we prayed for them and their friends through every season of life. We still do, even though our kids are now adults.

Our kids are our first and most important prayer assignment.

I doubt we will know the full fruit of those prayers until we reach Heaven, but I know without a doubt they had a significant impact on the lives of our kids. The fact that God answers prayer and rewards those who seek Him (see Hebrews 11:6) has been the foundation of my hope for my kids. No matter what they may face, my hope is steadfast in Him, for He is faithful.

Pause and Reflect…

> *Were you tempted to lose hope during a difficult season with your child?*
>
> *What did you do to keep from losing hope?*

It can be tempting to lose hope when we face difficult seasons with our children. However, we must hold onto the fact that what seems impossible to us is always possible with God. The Bible is full of stories of God coming through in impossible ways in impossible situations. It is His nature to be unhindered and unintimidated by human limitations. When Jesus met the rich young ruler who turned away because he had made money his idol, Jesus told His disciples it was easier for a camel to go through the eye of a needle than for a rich person to be saved. Yet, Jesus added, "With man this is impossible, but with God all things are possible" (Matthew 19:26).

When the angel Gabriel appeared to Mary and told her she would become pregnant with the son of God, Mary asked how that could happen. It was truly impossible. Yet, Gabriel pointed to a higher reality. The person of the Holy Spirit and the power of the Most High could make even this "impossibility" possible (see Luke 1:34–35).

Like Mary, today's children, teens, and young adults are highly favored by God. The Lord is with them, and the Holy Spirit is coming upon them to enable, empower, and strengthen them. For those who do not yet know Him, the Spirit is upon them to convict and convince them of their need for Jesus (see John 16:7–11 AMP).

When Zerubbabel felt inadequate for the task of rebuilding the temple, the prophet Zechariah brought him this word from God: "Not by might nor by power, but by my Spirit,' says the Lord Almighty. "What are you, mighty mountain? Before Zerubbabel you will become level ground. Then he will bring out the capstone to shouts of 'God bless it! God bless it!'" (Zechariah 4:6–7).

We can cling to the same promise. What seems too big for us is not too big for God. As we move forward in faith, declaring and praying God's promises over our children, we will see mountains leveled before us (see Matthew 21:21). We know that God's word is good, that His promises will not fail.

> *As the rain and the snow come down from heaven, and do not return to it without watering the earth and making it bud and flourish, so that it yields seed for the sower and bread for the eater, so is my word that goes out from my mouth: It will not return to me empty, but will accomplish what I desire and achieve the purpose for which I sent it.* (Isaiah 55:10–11)

The promises He has made over our children are destined for fulfillment. Our prayers of faith will nurture those seeds until they are ready to sprout and grow. He is the God of miracles. It is His will that our children all know Him as their Savior and walk in the fullness of their calling. We can and must partner with His will in prayer.

Our lives are not just about what will happen while we are alive. Our lives plant seeds into the future and create an inheritance for future generations. We are not living only for ourselves, but also for them. Our children are the future.

Powerful Parenting Insights

- ➢ It is our job to pray for them in ways they don't know how to pray.
- ➢ It is our job to birth things in the spirit on their behalf.
- ➢ It is our job (our joy and our privilege) to look into their future and declare the good purposes of God upon them.

They are an Elisha company, and they are destined for greatness.

Digging Deeper Workbook Chapter 9

Nothing is impossible with God. Not even the biggest hurdle can stop Him.

He is the God who stopped up the sea so the Israelites could cross. Read Exodus 14:16.

He is the God who made the sun stand still so the Israelites could win a battle. Read Joshua 10:1-15.

Read **Zechariah 4:6.**

> *"Not by might nor by power, but by my Spirit," says the* Lord.

Review these Powerful Parenting Insights:

Powerful Parenting Insights

➢ One of our main assignments as parents is to be spiritual shields for our children so they can walk through the enemy's attacks unharmed.
➢ We do this with our words, our love, and through prayer.

Review the Ephesians 6:10-20 list of weapons God has provided to help us do battle for our children against the attacks of the enemy.

Write them out and post them in your prayer closet so you will remember to use them every time you pray for your children.

Powerful Parenting Insights

➢ It is our job to pray for them in ways they don't know how to pray.
➢ It is our job to birth things in the spirit on their behalf.
➢ It is our job (our joy and our privilege) to look into their future and declare the good purposes of God upon them.

Read, Memorize, and Daily Declare Matthew 19:26.

> "With man this is impossible, but with God all things are possible."

Pray

Father God, I pray that just as Elisha received a double portion of Elijah's anointing when he watched Elijah ascend to Heaven in a whirlwind, so too may the whirlwind of the Holy Spirit bring this double portion of the anointing upon these young people. Lord, I declare these Elisha generations will do twice as much for the Kingdom as the generations before them. I believe history will be astounded by all they do for the Church and the world. Thank You, Lord, for anointing these generations to powerfully fulfill their calling and complete their assignment "Not by might nor by power, but by my Spirit," as You have declared over them, Lord.

Chapter 10

Grace for Revival

Since my daughter Danielle has been in Bible school, I have watched her rise into the prophetic, accompanied by a tremendous knowledge of the Scripture. She has also begun to move in supernatural healing. At times, she has tangibly felt the power of God flow through her to heal people. This is just the beginning. I believe God is training and preparing her for public ministry, and her life will impact multitudes. She has received prophecies declaring she will surpass me in ministry, and I believe it. It is my great joy to see her stepping into her calling and walking in a revival lifestyle. It is my prayer that each one of my children would surpass me in spiritual zeal, maturity, and anointing as they walk out their calling. That should be our goal, as parents.

I believe one of the main calls of the Millennial Generation and Generation Z is the call to birth revival. In the past, God has used certain generations to release a move of God on the earth—the Reformation, the Great Awakenings, the Welsh Revival, the Azusa Street Revival, and many others. Now, I believe the earth is ripe for another great move of God.

In his first book, Bill Johnson, the senior leader of Bethel Church in Redding, California, says he believes a great revival will be initiated by an "Elijah generation" that will transcend all other generations of Christians in regard to their ability to do great works of power.

Johnson believes momentum is already building toward this revival. He says, "I live for the revival that is unfolding and believe it will surpass all previous moves combined, bringing more than one billion souls into the Kingdom."[39]

This revival is beginning to be ushered in by the younger generations. Many, many young people and children are passionately pursuing the call of God on their lives and walking in incredible miracles and power. At Bethel Church, children learn how to prophesy and pray for the sick, and they regularly see miracles happen at the hands of kids. Many other churches are also beginning to disciple their children and young people in the things of the Spirit, and the results of their childlike faith mixed with Holy Spirit power are incredible. Yet, what we are seeing now is only the beginning of something that will be beyond what we can even ask or imagine.

We are intended to advance the Kingdom like a relay race, in which each generation goes successively farther because they are riding on their parents' momentum.

We are called to build the Kingdom like people built the great cathedrals of Europe during the Middle Ages. In the twelfth century, when cathedral building began, people possessed no great machinery to ease or speed the process. Those massive structures typically took several hundred years to build from concept to completion. A town would rally around the idea of building a cathedral for the glory of God, and many generations of workers would give years of their lives serving a vision they knew they would not see completed in their lifetime.

They would build for God and for future generations. This is a powerful perspective, and it is exactly what enabled people with so little technology to create such incredible buildings, many of which are still standing many hundreds of years later.

If we can adopt this same kind of cathedral thinking in our work of advancing the Kingdom of God on earth, I believe we too will see incredible and lasting results. Bill Johnson says, "I have great hopes and faith that our generation and the ones to follow will actually see, for the first time in history, revival that was not only sustained but increased in momentum in each following generation."[40]

Pause and Reflect on this vision and invitation God is setting before us as parents and grandparents.

> *Will I pass on what I have learned and support the rising generations as they begin to step into positions of leadership and influence?*
>
> *Will I believe in them, despite our differences from them?*
>
> *Is it my heart's desire to see this possibility become reality?*

Great Grace

How can we prevail in such dark and difficult times? Is the power of our prayers really adequate for the task? The answer is *yes!* God has given us what we need and increased the measure of grace in our lives to face any difficulties we may encounter. The apostle Paul says, *"where sin abounded, grace abounded much more"* (Romans 5:20 NKJV).

This means no matter how sinful the culture around us, God has given us more than enough grace to overcome and to bring the Kingdom into that environment. This means it doesn't matter how far our children have fallen away from Him. His grace in our lives is sufficient to pray them back into the Kingdom. We do not need to be afraid. We do not need to look at the blueprints and think, *This is impossible.* Instead, we can have hope because the darker it seems, the more God's divine enablement is available to us.

Powerful Parenting Insights

> ➢ God has destined us and our children to overcome.
> ➢ We can be confident as our children face more sinful environments and greater temptations than we did, they will also experience greater grace in their lives and ministries.
> ➢ Many of our children will boldly and faithfully proclaim the gospel to their peers and spark revival among the nations.

In Acts 4:33, it says the first generation of revivalists set the world on fire, "With great power the apostles continued to testify to the resurrection of the Lord Jesus. And God's grace was so powerfully at work in them all." Some other translations say, "great grace was upon them" (NKJV). God gave them great grace to persevere and to successfully spread the gospel throughout the known world.

In the span of about forty years, one small group of Jewish men and women spread this new belief about Jesus to all parts of the Roman Empire of that day. They did this without any of our modern technology through arduous journeys, handwritten letters, and preaching under persecution. Many of them did it by laying down their lives. When we really think about it, what the first-century believers accomplished is astounding. It was a cathedral of faith that paved the way for the growth of Christianity in the centuries that would follow.

Upon these rising generations, God has placed increased grace so they can accomplish His purposes for their lives and expand the Kingdom ever further. While this expansion of the Kingdom has been happening throughout history since the time of Jesus, I believe we are entering a season of acceleration and that today's young people have a truly special and dynamic calling upon their lives. I believe it will be in our day as it was prophesied by Habakkuk long ago.

> *"I am going to do something in your days that you would not believe, even if you were told."* (Habakkuk 1:5)

Technology Evangelism

One of the ways this will happen is through the power of technology. Those of us in the older generations are sometimes critical of the degree to which the Millennials and Generation Z use technology. While our concerns are not completely unfounded and a healthy balance is important, we must remember technology is also an incredible tool for the gospel. During the mid-1700s, in the height of the Methodist movement in England, John Wesley traveled by carriage or on horseback through all kinds of weather preaching five or more times a day, each time in a different town. If he wanted people to hear his message, he had to go to them personally. Though their technology was limited, Wesley, Whitfield, and other reformers had a tremendous impact in England and eventually throughout the Christian world.

Today, a person can travel across the world by airplane in just a few days. Books and other printed materials are very accessible and inexpensive. Sermons can be recorded and shared on the Internet and simultaneously reach people in the United States, Germany, Brazil, China, Kenya, and Papua New Guinea. In restricted nations, missionaries now have electronic versions of the Bible on flash drives or other small devices that can be more easily smuggled into places where it is not allowed. We are so used to this reality that we can forget how incredible it is. We can lose sight of its potential to completely change the spiritual landscape of the world in just a generation.

Peter Guirguis, who runs an evangelism-themed website called *Not Ashamed of the Gospel*, gives these five reasons why he believes evangelism online will play a significant role in the future of evangelism:

1. Technology is extremely affordable. Even in the poorest nations of the world, many people have smartphones and laptops.
2. Internet evangelism can reach millions of people. There is no limit to how many people could view something posted online.
3. It's cheap, especially when compared to the cost of massive crusades and other large evangelistic events.
4. People love to share articles, videos, and quotes that have impacted them online. This multiplies our impact passed just our own friend and acquaintance circles to reach people we do not know.
5. Non-Christians are searching for God. (Literally, they are googling God.)[41]

Every day, a person has the potential to impact any number of their "friends" or "followers" online through what they post or tweet. This impact can have a ripple effect when people share or retweet a post, enabling it to reach complete strangers.

I know a young woman who has a significant ministry to other women, particularly those who are survivors of abuse, and she does this ministry primarily through private groups or private messaging on social media sites. Many of the women she ministers to are people she has never met in person, yet they have reached out to her because they read her tweets advocating for women in abusive situations. The internet can feel like a safe place to be real, and this young woman is finding that many women are feeling safe to tell her things they cannot tell their own family members.

Another young woman, who is a passionate evangelist with a strong healing gift, regularly posts testimonies of people being healed.

She also posts words of knowledge online and people often respond, saying they were healed when they read her word of knowledge. Her testimonies encourage others to also be bold in praying for the sick and sharing the gospel wherever they go.

Using live video programs like Facebook Live or Periscope, a young dad and his elementary-age daughter are able to give prophetic words to people all over the world. Some of these people are complete strangers who just happen to click on their videos out of curiosity. The possibilities for ministry online are nearly endless. Truly, the Internet contains a field of people that is ripe for harvest.

Even after people are saved, technology creates a space for more effective discipleship, communication, and community-building within the Church at large.[42] Our lives are busy, and technology makes it easier for us to connect. We can shoot a friend a text or comment on a Facebook post in the time it takes to sit at a red light. We can create Facebook groups for prayers requests and testimonies. We can use apps like Voxer, Marco Polo, and Snapchat for back-and-forth voice and video communication. We can listen to podcasts of sermons online while we commute to work or wash the dishes. In these ways and many more, technology can help us grow as believers and as friends, and it can help us reach the lost and bring them into a place of belonging and discipleship.

Pause and Reflect…

> *Am I taking advantage of all this technology to help spread the gospel even to those I have never met?*
>
> *Am I encouraging my children to do this as well?*

Technology is an incredible tool for evangelism, relationship, and discipleship, and it is one that the rising generations are not only comfortable with, but that they have at their fingertips continually.

Powerful Parenting Insights

- As their parents and grandparents, we must believe in and pray for an incredible outcome.
- Our kids are destined to be revivalists and are called and equipped to be evangelists online and in their everyday lives, spreading the gospel of love to a world that is literally at their fingertips.
- Let's partner with God in pointing our kids toward incredible things—even if it looks different in their generations than it did in ours.

A Word for Our Children

About a year ago, God gave me a clear word about this coming revival and our role as parents in it. This word came to me while I was speaking at the Merge Event with Yolanda Stith on August 25, 2016. It is long, but I share it here to build our faith for what God wants to do through us and through our kids. His plans are so much greater than many of us have realized! Here is what God said to me that day:

> Everything I have given you has come from My hands. I have a call, and I have a plan, and I have a strategy to take your children and bring them into another dimension of Me. Didn't I say in My Word that your sons and your daughters would prophesy? And so it will be. It will be said of your children like was said of the early church: "Those who have turned the world upside down have come here also." The enemy sees it, and therefore, there is a

great war against their destiny. There is a great war against what I desire to do in this next generation.

So, I am calling upon you to stand in the gap. I am calling upon you to lift up your voice, for you have power and authority over all the works of darkness. As you stand and as you pray and as you intercede, nothing will by any means harm them. So, pray and stand and watch. Be sober and be vigilant. Your adversary the devil goes about as a roaring lion, seeking to take them out, but you know better. The spirit of seeing and knowing is in many of the fathers and mothers in this day, and that's why I trained so many of you in the prophetic—so stir up the gifts I placed within you. Lift your eyes and look and see, because I desire to do great and mighty things in and among this generation, and so it will be. You will stand, and you will watch, and you will give birth to that which I have called them to be and do.

Don't grow weary in well-doing. Don't look to the left. Don't look to the right. Look unto Me. I am the author. I am the finisher of that which I have called them to be and do. And I *will* perfect everything that concerns your sons and your daughters in this generation of young people that I am raising up. Yes, I am raising them up! But I am also raising you up and perfecting everything in your souls that would hinder you from being all that I have called you to be in their lives so that your prayers are not hindered. I need you to be healed and whole. So, this day I am strengthening you by My Spirit in the inner person, in your core, and you can sense Me strengthening you. You can sense Me working in you, and it's not just for you. It's on behalf of what I desire to do in and among your children and this generation of youth.

I see an army rising up, and it's an army of young men and young women, those who are called and ordained to live in a time such as this. The enemy is seeing that they're arising, and he is afraid of them. The enemy knows things about the realm of the spirit that some of My people don't know about the realm of the spirit. He sees that they are rising up—little Joshuas, little Jeremiahs, little Calebs, little Marys, little Deborahs. I see many, many, many more ministry gifts than in any other generation. They are called and anointed with ministry gifts because where sin abounds, My grace is going to do so much more to abound. I am anointing them, and many signs and wonders will follow them.

They need grace, so I am calling you to seek My face, and I'm calling you to stand in the gap like you've never stood in the gap before so that there are no surprises. I am going to teach you how to pray. I am going to teach you how to war. I'm going to teach you how to go in until you have a breakthrough on behalf of those whom I have called you to watch over. I've called you to watch over them and to stand in the gap for them, and you will say yes because of your love and your heart for your children and this generation. Remember, I have said in My Word that if you are willing and obedient you will eat the good of the land.

There is great sorrow when your children are bowed down like the woman who was crippled by a spirit for eighteen years. She was bent over and could not straighten up, and there was great sorrow. But when you pray, I hear you, and they are released and set free from their bondages. Just don't be moved by what you see. Don't be moved by what you hear. You must only be moved by one thing and one thing alone—the fact that all the promises of God are yes and amen, and all of your children will be taught of the Lord and great will be the peace, or the undisturbed composure, of your children.

Our children are anointed with fresh oil, and they are destined to carry the torch of revival fire, but they can't do it alone. They need us to believe in them and to fight for them in the Spirit. The final section of this book is all about how we can do that effectively.

Digging Deeper Workbook Chapter 10

Read Haggai 2:9.

> *"The glory of this present house will be greater than the glory of the former house.... And in this place I will grant peace."*
>
> *What does this mean to you and your immediate family, your spiritual children, and your church family concerning revival for the next generations?*

Review these Powerful Parenting Insights:

Powerful Parenting Insights

- **God has destined us and our children to overcome.**
  What are you and your children needing to overcome to move forward with your missions?

- **We can be confident as our children face more sinful environments and greater temptations than we did, they will also experience greater grace in their lives and ministries.**
  Why do you have this confidence?

- **Many of our children will boldly and faithfully proclaim the gospel to their peers and spark revival among the nations.**
  How are you praying for your children to help them become part of God's kingdom plan for this revival?

Powerful Parenting Insights

> ➤ As their parents and grandparents, we must believe in and pray for an incredible outcome.
> *Pray for God to protect your children and grandchildren, particularly from all the attacks and temptations that come through the Internet.*

> ➤ Our kids are destined to be revivalists and are called and equipped to be evangelists online and in their everyday lives, spreading the gospel of love to a world that is literally at their fingertips.
> *What are you seeing happening as your children use these tools to evangelize their world?*

> ➤ Let's partner with God in pointing our kids toward incredible things—even if it looks different in their generations than it did in ours.
> *How are you partnering with God?*
> *How are you going to increase this in your prayer life?*

Read, Memorize, and Daily Declare this word from God in Habakkuk 1:5.

> *"I am going to do something in your days that you would not believe, even if you were told."*

Read God's instructions and then write your own specific prayer for your children.

> So, pray and stand and watch. Be sober and be vigilant. Your adversary the devil goes about as a roaring lion,

seeking to take them out, but you know better. Don't grow weary in well-doing. Don't look to the left. Don't look to the right. Look unto Me. I am the author. I am the finisher of that which I have called them to be and do. And I *will* perfect everything that concerns your sons and your daughters in this generation of young people that I am raising up. They need grace, so I am calling you to seek My face, and I'm calling you to stand in the gap like you've never stood in the gap before so that there are no surprises. I am going to teach you how to pray. I am going to teach you how to war. I'm going to teach you how to go in until you have a breakthrough on behalf of those whom I have called you to watch over. I've called you to watch over them and to stand in the gap for them, and you will say yes because of your love and your heart for your children and this generation.

Your Prayer:

Chapter 11
The Power to Pray

Now that we have examined God's very high value for children and the calling He has placed on the lives of the upcoming generations, it is time for us to learn how to pray.

> **As parents, the most important question we can ask ourselves is,**
> *Are we preparing the way for our children in the spirit?*

We can provide abundantly for our children and meet all their physical needs yet leave them malnourished in the spirit. As parents, our responsibility is not to just provide outwardly, but to provide for and support our kids in spiritual ways as well. If we want them to reach their full potential and the destiny God created them for, spiritual support is the most important gift we can give our children. When we become intercessors and warriors in prayer on their behalf, we set them up for true prosperity in life and spirit.

Part of living in this world is experiencing pain and disappointment. This will be true until Jesus returns. Jesus acknowledged this when He said, "In this world you will have trouble. But take heart! I have overcome the world" (John 16:33). The fact that we pray for our children does not mean nothing bad will ever happen to them.

> "The Bible assures us that our prayers play a vital part in keeping trouble from them. And when a painful thing does happen, they will be protected in the midst of it so it will be to their betterment and not their destruction."
> – Stormie Omartian"[43]

Our prayers make a tangible difference. If we pray for our children regularly, we will see the fruit of it in their lives. A friend of mine learned this when his daughter, soon after graduating college, decided that bartending was a good career choice. He felt angry and disappointed. On nights when she worked, she didn't come home until 2 a.m., and her father found himself worrying constantly and struggling to sleep until she arrived home. One night, he had to drop her off at work because of trouble with her car, so he decided to check out the place and meet her boss. It turned out to be the dingiest low-life bar he had ever been in.

Following that discovery, my friend asked the men he regularly met with on Sunday mornings to pray. During a time of sharing, one of the men quoted Matthew 11:28–30, where Jesus says, "Come to me, all you who are weary and burdened, and I will give you rest. Take my yoke upon you and learn from me, for I am gentle and humble in heart, and you will find rest for your souls. For my yoke is easy and my burden is light."

At that moment, my friend realized a yoke is a tool designed to make whatever one is doing easier. He said to the Lord, "I've been doing this my own way, and You are offering me tools. What should I do?"

God answered by giving him three strategies:

1. Don't worry.
2. Pray.
3. Speak words of life into her.

Starting that day, worry ceased to be an issue in my friend's life, and he was able to sleep. He regularly prayed, made declarations over her life, and encouraged her to pursue Jesus. Eventually, she did just that. She abandoned bartending and is still pursuing God today. All this happened because my friend realized the power of prayer. The solution wasn't worrying or fear. It wasn't in trying to strong-arm her into a better choice. The solution was finding rest in Jesus and praying for his daughter from that place of peace.

Kathryn Kuhlman once said that the greatest power given to any individual is the power of prayer. I like to put it this way: The greatest power given to any parent is the power of prayer!

Powerful Parenting Insights

- ➢ **Our intercession for our children is the most powerful tool in our parenting repertoire.**
- ➢ **Prayer transcends the effect of our parenting mistakes and the negative influences on our kids' lives.**
- ➢ **Prayer has tremendous power to change hearts and transform situations. It can do what human strength cannot.**
- ➢ **Prayer is an essential part of helping our children reach their full potential in life.**
- ➢ **When we support them in prayer, we open the door for God to work powerfully in their lives.**

> "Prayer is simple, prayer is supernatural, and to anyone not related to our Lord Jesus Christ, prayer is apt to look stupid." - Oswald Chambers[44]

Mark Batterson, the author of *Praying Circles around Your Children*, has this encouragement for the praying parent:

> You'll never be a perfect parent, but you can be a praying parent. Prayer is your highest privilege as a parent... Prayer turns ordinary parents into prophets who shape the destinies of their children, grandchildren, and every generation that follows...Your prayers for your children are the greatest legacy you can leave.[45]

Too many parents walk through life feeling helpless in the face of the hurdles in their children's lives. *What can I do that would actually be enough in this situation,* they wonder? The answer is prayer. We have what we need to help our children turn their lives toward God. Hidden in the simple act of prayer is an incredibly powerful tool. It is more than wishful thinking or a shot in the dark. Prayer is a powerful reality that can change the course of our children's lives.

Proof for Prayer

We believe this by faith because it is what God tells us in His Word, but science is also beginning to prove the power of prayer. In quantum physics, the law of entanglement says that relationship is the defining characteristic of everything in space and time.[46] In other words, we are all interconnected in a way that transcends physical closeness. The Bible tells us the same thing in Romans 12:5, "So in Christ we, though many, form one body, and each member belongs to all the others."

What we do, say, and think impacts one another in a way that often does not seem to make sense. Those of us who are spiritually sensitive have known this to be true through our own experiences. We have felt it when we walked into a room where a depressed stranger sat, and we suddenly felt terribly heavy and sad. We have felt the contagious power of another person's hope or joy. We have felt the shift in our mindsets and emotions as others prayed for us. This is all experiential evidence for this scientific and spiritual reality of entanglement.

God has so embedded this spiritual reality in the fabric of our world that even unbelieving scientists are beginning to discover it. The law of entanglement is scientific proof that prayer does work. It demonstrates on a molecular level that "the prayer of a righteous person is powerful and effective" (James 5:16).

According to Dr. Caroline Leaf, "Our intentions can alter not only our own DNA molecules, but the DNA molecules of others as well."[47] Our prayers can actually cause a change in another person's mind. Research has shown that "even thirty seconds a day of direct heartfelt intention will cumulatively alter not only your own destiny, but impact the lives of others in this generation and the next three at least."[48] This is an incredible discovery and it confirms what the Bible has told us all along! Our prayers, when fueled by faith in God, are powerful agents of change in our lives and in the lives of others.

Foundations of Prayer

Why can we pray? These three simple spiritual truths will build our faith as praying parents, so our prayers will be powerfully effective.

1. We Have Authority

> "If prayer puts God to work on earth, then by the same token, prayerlessness rules God out of the world's affairs, and prevents Him from working." – E.M. Bounds[49]

When God created Adam and Eve, He gave them authority over the earth, to fill and subdue it (see Genesis 2). They were ambassadors for God's Kingdom on planet earth with actual authority to rule, as we see in the fact that God invited Adam to name the animals He created.

When Adam and Eve decided to rebel against God, they actually gave their authority over the earth to Satan (see 2 Corinthians 4:4, Luke 4:6).

When Jesus came as the "second Adam" (see 1 Corinthians 15:45–47), He came to put right all that went wrong in the Garden. In answer to the problem of sin, He offered forgiveness of sin and new creation life. In answer to humanity's loss of authority, Jesus stripped the devil of his power and restored authority over the earth to those who believe in Him (see Colossians 2:13–15). This means believers now have the authority to command the devil to stop harassing people or causing negative circumstances. The devil still lives in this world and still seeks to "kill, steal, and destroy," (John 10:10). He is here as a usurper and rebel, and when Christ returns in the future, He will remove his influence from the earth. Until that time, we live in a dual reality. Jesus has all authority in Heaven and on earth, and He has given that authority to us (see Matthew 28:18–20; Ephesians 1:20–22). Yet, our enemy still roams the earth, and unbelievers are still under his influence (see 1 John 5:19).

With this in mind, we can view our position here on earth as enforcers of God's Kingdom rule. Jesus won the victory in the spirit realm, and now it is our job to enforce that victory in our lives and in the lives of those around us. Even before Jesus died on the cross, He gave His disciples authority over evil spirits (see Mark 6:7). This was their first commissioning into ministry before they had been filled with the Spirit. Now, on the other side of the cross, our authority over the devil and his works is guaranteed. Yet, many believers do not walk in this authority simply because they are unaware of it.

The fact is, if we want to experience victory in life, we must take authority over our lives, and we must ask our Father for the good gifts He has provided for us. The same is true in the lives of our children. The enemy is not going to just lay down and give up because we have authority over him. He is a liar, and he doesn't play by the rules. He's like a criminal who is sneaking around and breaking the law, and he won't stop until someone who has authority makes him stop. That someone is every one of us.

Prayer is important because it is our partnership with God in exercising His authority on earth. God is in charge (He has all authority), but He does not control everything. He is like the King of a country who has absolute authority but who does not control every action of his subjects. People can still disobey an earthly king, and they are free to disobey God. We might think it'd be better if God just controlled everything so nothing bad ever happened, but He wants a more dynamic relationship with us than such an arrangement would allow. He wants us to live with Him in freedom and love and to be His powerful partners in His Kingdom work.

Powerful Parenting Insights

- If we think, *whatever happens will happen, and it's God's will,* we are shirking our duty.
- As believers, we are called to affect the course and destiny of our children through prayer.

One of the primary ways that we exercise our authority on earth is by inviting the Father to act according to His will. In other words, we ask Him to do what He has promised to do. Some people think we do not need to ask since God has already provided everything we need through the cross, but the Bible clearly tells us that asking is important. Asking is an important part of walking in our authority on earth. We don't have to understand why it is true to believe that it is true. The apostle James put it this way: "You do not have because you do not ask God" (James 4:2). Believing that we have authority and acting on that authority through asking is the first foundation for faith-filled prayer.

2. God Hears Our Prayers.

The second foundation is the belief that when we ask, God hears us. As the apostle John said, "This is the confidence we have in approaching God: that if we ask anything according to his will, he hears us" (1 John 5:14). This confidence births faith and boldness in our hearts. We are not pleading with a deaf or uncaring deity. We are speaking with our attentive and loving Father. "For the eyes of the Lord are on the righteous and his ears are attentive to their prayer" (1 Peter 3:12). When we speak, He pays attention. He listens to every word.

Jesus illustrated this for us when He stood at the tomb of Lazarus. All odds were against Him. The people around Him were full of fear, doubt, and disappointment. Jesus grieved along with them. He loved Lazarus deeply. He had an emotional connection just as we do with our children. Yet, He was not overwhelmed by His emotions because He knew His Father would hear Him when He prayed. Jesus knew who He was (a man with spiritual authority) and who His Father was (a kind and attentive God), therefore, He had the boldness to overcome His grief and to publicly pray for a miracle. In fact, in His prayer, He announced His confidence that God always hears His prayers.

> *Father, I thank you that you have heard me. I knew that you always hear me, but I said this for the benefit of the people standing here, that they may believe that you sent me.* (John 11:41–42)

Jesus wanted everyone there to know that the Father listened when He prayed. Then, He stood at the tomb of Lazarus, who had been dead four days, and commanded him back to life.

We can pray with the same confidence that Jesus modeled in this story because we come to the Father in Jesus' name. We come to Him as forgiven and adopted children in His family, as brothers and sisters to Jesus, and through Him, we enter into the same authority and privilege in relationship with the Father (see Hebrews 10:19–20; 2 Corinthians 5:17–21).

> "*Let us then approach God's throne of grace with confidence, so that we may receive mercy and find grace to help us in our time of need.*" (Hebrews 4:16)

We can come to the Father boldly because we have right standing with Him, and He promises to always hear our prayers.

One of my closest friends told me a story about her son that illustrates this well. When he was in college, one day he told her that she had ruined him in his mind because everything she said was about God, and he was tired of hearing it. He told her she had screwed him up, and then he left the house very upset. My friend knew her son was taking a trip to New York City that day, and when he left she prayed, "Lord, he's in your hands." Then she asked God to send other believers across his path to testify of His love and goodness. My friend did not need to wait long to see that God had heard her prayer. When her son came home, he said, "You are not going to believe what happened!" He then told her that he had met a girl on the train, and the girl had started talking to him about Jesus. "I can't get away from it," he said, but he wasn't angry anymore. That simple encounter and answer to prayer was a turning point for him, and now he thanks his mom for the way she raised him. My friend had absolute confidence that God heard her when she prayed.

3. God Answers Our Prayers.

The third foundation builds on the second. Not only does God hear our prayers, but He also answers our prayers. God promises us, "Call to me and I will answer you and tell you great and unsearchable things you do not know" (Jeremiah 33:3). In 1 John 5:14, John assures us God hears us when we pray. He follows that with this promise: "And if we know that he hears us—whatever we ask—we know that we have what we asked of him" (1 John 5:15). We do not always receive the answers to our prayer immediately, but that does not mean that God has not heard or that He will not answer. Instead, when we find ourselves waiting to see the manifestation of what we've prayed for, it is an opportunity to stand in faith. It is a time to trust in what we know to be true—that God does hear and does answer—and hold to that truth in faith even before we see it with our eyes.

When we pray, our prayers ascend before God as an invitation to act on our behalf. God responds by releasing the spiritual breakthrough or provision we need, but sometimes we do not see the manifestation of it immediately. There are various reasons for this. The Bible tells us that the answers to our prayers can be hindered by a spiritual attack (see Daniel 10). The enemy often does not give up easily. In these situations, we must "imitate those who through faith and patience inherit what has been promised" (Hebrews 6:12) and persevere in prayer. The good news is, when we pray, use the name of Jesus, our authority in Christ is released, and therefore, the enemy must release his influence over our children. Our job is to then stand firm in faith until the devil admits his defeat.

The answers to our prayers can also be hindered by our children's free will. They may choose to resist the whisperings of God in their hearts for a season, even though He is actively drawing them to Him. In my own life, I vividly remember the conviction I experienced for a year before I got saved. I had walked away from God in my teen years. After my mother became involved in the Catholic charismatic movement, she and two of her friends began praying for me. Because of that, I came under tremendous conviction from the Holy Spirit. Even secular music seemed to point me to Jesus—especially the song "Show Me the Way" by Peter Framptom. One night, as I drove home from a party, I heard this song, and I tangibly felt a spiritual tug-of-war over my life. I felt God pulling me on one side to come to Him, and on the other side, I felt a dark force pulling me in the other direction. The warfare was real, and I knew it. Even still, it took me an entire year to answer God's call. I am glad my mother didn't assume God wasn't answering her prayers when I stubbornly resisted the Spirit's conviction.

At other times, we do not know exactly why we experience a delay in getting answers. What we do know is God is not holding out on us. The problem is not on His end. He is the God who answers prayer. The solution to "unanswered" prayer is to believe God is answering and to persevere in faith, even when we don't understand. The unseen spiritual realm is more real than the visible physical realm, and sometimes what we see in the natural does not yet reflect God's eternal reality. It is also important to point out that sometimes when we pray in faith and perseverance, things may get a whole lot worse before it gets better. This is why Paul tells us, "So we fix our eyes not on what is seen, but on what is unseen, since what is seen is temporary, but what is unseen is eternal" (2 Corinthians 4:18).

Prayer is a powerful force, more powerful than many of us realize, and it has the potential to forever change the course of the lives of our children. The apostle James, when talking about the power of intercession, recalled the story of Elijah, a normal human like us who stopped the rain for three and a half years and then caused it to rain again—all through the power of prayer. This is the legacy we are stepping into when we decide to pray the prayer of intercession.

> *The heartfelt and persistent prayer of a righteous man (believer) can accomplish much [when put into action and made effective by God—it is dynamic and can have tremendous power].* (James 5:16 AMP)

Powerful Parenting Insights

- Prayer is the most powerful tool we have received as believers and parents.
- Prayer can change the landscape and the climate of our families.
- Prayer can open closed doors and welcome the work of the Spirit in the lives of our children.
- Truly, the greatest gift we can give to our children is the choice to pray for them—to be intercessors and warriors on their behalf.

Digging Deeper Workbook Chapter 11

Prayer is important because it is our partnership with God in exercising His authority on earth. Read and meditate on these scriptures concerning the foundations of prayer we studied in this chapter. Record how each one impacts your prayers.

1. We Have Authority.

James 4:2
Matthew 18:19
John 14:13
John 15:16
John 16:23
Matthew 7:11
Matthew 7:7

2. God Hears Our Prayers.

1 John 5:14

1 Peter 3:12
Hebrews 10:19–20
2 Corinthians 5:17–21

3. God Answers Our Prayers.

1 John 5:15
Jeremiah 33:3

Review these Powerful Parenting Insights:

Powerful Parenting Insights

- ➢ **Our intercession for our children is the most powerful tool in our parenting repertoire.**
  Am I consistently using this powerful tool?

- ➢ **Prayer transcends the effect of our parenting mistakes and the negative influences on our kids' lives.**
  Thank God for this powerful truth.

- ➢ **Prayer has tremendous power to change hearts and transform situations. It can do what human strength cannot.**
  Declare this in your life and the lives of your children daily.

- ➢ **Prayer is an essential part of helping our children reach their full potential in life.**
- ➢ **When we support them in prayer, we open the door for God to work powerfully in their lives.**

Powerful Parenting Insights

- ➤ If we think, *whatever happens will happen, and it's God's will*, we are shirking our duty.
- ➤ As believers, we are called to affect the course and destiny of our children through prayer.

Powerful Parenting Insights

- ➤ Prayer can change the landscape and the climate of our families.
- ➤ Prayer can open closed doors and welcome the work of the Spirit in the lives of our children.
- ➤ Truly, the greatest gift we can give to our children is the choice to pray for them—to be intercessors and warriors on their behalf.

God has given us these three strategies:

1. Don't worry.
2. Pray.
3. Speak words of life into your child.

Read, Memorize, and Daily Declare James 5:16.

> *The heartfelt and persistent prayer of a righteous man (believer) can accomplish much [when put into action and made effective by God—it is dynamic and can have tremendous power].* (AMP)

Pray

Father God, I want to experience victory in life. I now know that means I must take the authority You have given me and exercise in my life and over the lives of my child. Thank You for the good gifts and tools You have provided for me as I pray daily for my child. I am aware the enemy is not going to just lay down and give up because he is a liar, and he doesn't play by the rules. He's like a criminal who is sneaking around and breaking the law, and he won't stop until someone who has authority makes him stop. Thank You that You have given me the tools I need so can be that someone.

Chapter 12

Prayer Alerts

A friend of mine experienced a parenting nightmare when her eighteen-year-old daughter decided to run away with a bad-news boyfriend. Like any parents would, she and her husband felt hurt and afraid, but they intentionally asked God how they should pray. They chose not to give in to anger or fear but to seek the Father's wisdom instead. God answered and directed them to release Hebrews 4:12 over all four of their children, including the one who had run away.

> *For the word of God is alive and active. Sharper than any double-edged sword, it penetrates even to dividing soul and spirit, joints and marrow; it judges the thoughts and attitudes of the heart.* (Hebrews 4:12)

So, this friend declared out loud over her children that God's Word is quick and powerful and sharper than any two-edged sword, separating spirit and soul. As she did, she felt God's Spirit direct her to bind any soul control and release the sword of God's Word to cut that control. She sensed that her children were bound in unhealthy relationships with soul ties that prevented them from being free to pursue God. In response, she prayed to break these soul ties and free her children in the spirit. Within a short period of time, three of her four children completely cut off their unhealthy relationships, including the eighteen-year-old daughter, who returned home. What an incredible testimony to the power of interceding for our children.

When Jesus was about to go to the cross, He warned Peter of a spiritual attack that would come against him (Luke 22:31-32). Jesus prayed for Peter that his faith would stay strong and that when he had overcome, he would then strengthen the other disciples. Jesus prayed for Peter and then spoke into his destiny with confidence that Peter would run his spiritual race and be everything he was called to be. This is a perfect example of the power of intercession to defeat the plans of the enemy and call forth destiny in the lives of others.

Intercession Defined

The Bible tells us there are all different kinds of prayer (see Ephesians 6:18 AMP). When we pray for our kids, we are using the prayer of intercession. We see an example of this in God's words to the prophet Ezekiel. "I looked for someone among them who would build up the wall and stand before me in the gap on behalf of the land..." (Ezekiel 22:30). From this, we see that an intercessor is one who builds up a wall of protection in the spirit. To stand in the gap implies closing up the hole in the wall so the enemy cannot get in. When we intercede for others, it is often because the spiritual walls in their lives have holes giving the enemy access and allowing him to harass them. As an intercessor, we can spiritually take a stand in that broken place and forbid the enemy from entering.

An intercessor is also a mediator—one who is a go-between to bring reconciliation and harmony between two parties (see Job 9:32–33). Sometimes, when we intercede for others, we come before God as His favored children and ask Him to pour out blessing and provision upon those who are not walking with Him or have strayed from Him. We come on their behalf and invite God to invade their lives with His goodness and love (even if they are not asking for it).

The role of the mediator or intercessor in prayer was prevalent in the Old Testament in the lives of Abraham, Moses, David, Samuel, Hezekiah, Elijah, Jeremiah, Ezekiel, and Daniel. Under the Old Covenant, not everyone had access to God, so God called the leaders, priests, and prophets of Israel to intercede on behalf of the people. In the New Covenant, that has changed. Now, we all have access to God through Jesus, who is the ultimate intercessor.

Jesus forever closed the gap between us and God when He died on the cross. In Hebrews, it says that Jesus has a perfect and eternal priesthood, unlike the priests of old, and because of this, "He is able to save completely those who come to God through him, because he always lives to intercede for them" (Hebrews 7:25). His priesthood, which is an act of intercession, lasts forever. He has bridged the gap for all time, so we can now intercede in prayer on behalf of others. As believers, we have equal authority in prayer and equal access to the Father (see Hebrews 7:24–25; Galatians 2:20). We are empowered to pray by the Holy Spirit, and our prayers will produce miracles (see Acts 1:8).

Powerful Parenting Insights

> When we stand in the gap for our children, we are releasing the ministry of Jesus and agreeing with what God has already said about their destiny.
> When we do this, in the spirit we are laying one hand on them and one hand on God as explained in Job 9:32-33.
> As we continue steadfastly, unmovable in persistent intercession, we are pulling our children out of spiritual darkness and toward the Kingdom of light.

You will pray to Him, and He will hear you, and you will pay your vows. You will also decide and decree a thing, and it will be established for you; and the light [of God's favor] will shine upon your ways. When you are cast down and humbled, you will speak with confidence, and the humble person He will lift up and save. He will even rescue the one [for whom you intercede] who is not innocent; and he will be rescued through the cleanness of your hands. (Job 22:27–30 AMP)

What an incredible thought—that through our prayers God will rescue others, even if they don't deserve it. God said this to Job even before the old covenant existed, and it is even more true now that we live under grace. When we pray, we are opening the connection and becoming the conduit for God's work in our children's lives—even if they are not seeking Him.

God is a just and loving God, and it is His will that all people come into a relationship with Him and learn to walk in freedom and maturity (see I Timothy 2:4). However, in this life, we sometimes face hurdles to God's will for our lives. These can result from our own choices, from our circumstances, from the choices of others, and from demonic attacks. It's important to note that the hard things in life do not come from God, but from the enemy (see John 10:10).

As intercessors, when we see these hurdles in the lives of our kids, it is our job to invite God, the righteous judge, to bring justice on behalf of our children and to right the wrongs the enemy has brought against them. God's will is that we would all be free of the enemy's attacks and walk in His blessing.

When we intercede for our children, we are setting in motion the will of God in their lives.

The prayer of intercession is one of the most powerful prayers mentioned in the Word of God. As we pray the scriptures and promises of God over others, we are praying the will of God into their lives! We are also praying for them to have open and obedient hearts. When we agree with God's purpose and plan for our children in prayer, we access tremendous spiritual power. "The earnest (heartfelt, continued) prayer of a righteous man makes tremendous power available [dynamic in its working]" (James 5:16 AMP). This is something we can do daily, whether we are physically with our children or not. There is no time or distance in the spirit. In fact, intercession often happens in the secret place of prayer, where only God sees and hears. Jesus promised, "…Your Father, who sees what is done in secret, will reward you" (Colossians 2:5; Matthew 6:6). So, no matter where we are when we pray, our prayers have the power to impact others.

The law of entanglement in quantum physics confirms that our prayers from a distance can have a real impact. Scientists believe our thoughts (including prayers) move faster than the speed of light, so physical distance is not a hindrance to our intercession.[50] No matter where our children may be, we can reach them in prayer, and we can release the will of God in their lives. This is an incredible truth—one that should birth hope in our hearts. No matter how far our children have strayed from God or how difficult their circumstances might be, we can touch them in prayer.

Pause and Reflect…

> *Tell yourself daily, no matter how far your children have strayed from God or how difficult their circumstances might be, you can touch them in prayer.*

Truly, intercession is a great demonstration of love, and that is why we parents are so qualified to do it for our children. Our hearts are naturally gripped with a deep love and compassion for our kids, and we selflessly serve them in many natural ways. When we translate this human love into the spiritual realm and use it as a force for prayer, our prayers begin to echo the supernatural love of Christ. After all, God loves our children even more than we do. In love-fueled intercession, we truly lay down our lives for others in prayer.

> **When we connect our natural love
> To the supernatural grace of God in intercession,
> we will have the strength to persevere in prayer
> until breakthrough comes.**

Praying with Importunity

Another word for persevering in prayer is *importunity*. Praying with importunity is an important part of intercession. Jesus made that very clear. As the great intercessor, He is the authority on prayer. In Luke 11, He taught His disciples some important lessons on prayer. First, He gave them the prayer we now call the Lord's Prayer, which is a prayer of supplication for one's own needs (see Luke 11:1–4). The only part of this prayer I will mention here is the beginning, *"Our Father."* Jesus told the disciples to pray to the Father in the name of Jesus (see John 14:6, 13). The name of Jesus not only has power and authority over Satan and his kingdom, but His name also gives us access to the throne of God. Jesus made this clear.

> *In that day you will no longer ask me anything. Very truly I tell you, my Father will give you whatever you ask in my name. Until now you have not asked for anything in my name. Ask and you will receive, and your joy will be complete.* (John 16:23–24)

When we pray for ourselves or for others, we must always pray to the Father in the name of Jesus. As intercessors, we align ourselves with the great intercessor by praying in His name. After Jesus taught the disciples the Lord's Prayer, He then told them a parable about intercession.

> *Suppose you have a friend, and you go to him at midnight and say, "Friend, lend me three loaves of bread; a friend of mine on a journey has come to me, and I have no food to offer him." And suppose the one inside answers, "Don't bother me. The door is already locked, and my children and I are in bed. I can't get up and give you anything." I tell you, even though he will not get up and give you the bread because of friendship, yet because of your shameless audacity he will surely get up and give you as much as you need.* (Luke 11:5–8)

In this parable, we approach the friend on behalf of another friend who is on a journey and has come to us in need. This request is not for us, which means it is a request of intercession. We are coming on behalf of another. This friend is staying at our house and is, therefore, our responsibility. We do not have what is needed to help this friend, so we petition our friend with a specific request—three loaves. We know exactly what we need.

For our purposes here, this second friend is a metaphor for our children. These children are our responsibility. They are under our care and authority, and we are intercessors for them. The journey symbolizes the journey of life they are on. At times, we as parents will feel like we don't know how to help our kids. We don't have the "three loaves" they need. When we have done all we know to do in the natural to help our children and they are still struggling, we must turn to the One who can help. We must become intercessors on their behalf.

Jesus shows us how to respond when it feels like our prayers are not being answered. Sometimes, it may seem as though God is not listening or caring, but that is not the truth. Intercessors know this and refuse to be shaken by what they may see or feel in the natural. Instead, they hold to the promises of God in His Word and continue to ask.

In the parable, the friend initially does not want to be troubled because it is the middle of the night, and he is already in bed. This symbolizes any resistance that may come against our prayers in the form of spiritual warfare. This is **not** how our Father responds to us because He is always eager to help. However, sometimes our answers are delayed for other reasons. Here Jesus shows us how to respond when it feels like our prayers are not being answered. God's Word does not lie, and it never fails. We can rely on God to fulfill all He has promised in the Bible. In fact, God gives us above and beyond what we asked for (see Ephesians 3:20)! Jesus says we receive the help we need because of our importunity or persistence. This is an essential quality of the prayer of intercession.

Webster's Dictionary defines the word *importunity* as "persistence in solicitation." The prayer of intercession is different from other types of prayer. Jesus' main point in His parable is that intercessors never quit praying until they see the answer they are seeking. We must not quit when we do not see visible results. The breakthrough may come quickly, or it may take years, but regardless, if we refuse to give up, our prayers will work.

Intercession involves persisting in prayer for another person *until* the breakthrough comes (see Luke 18:1).

[Note that the Digging Deeper Workbook section for this chapter and chapter 13 is at the end of chapter 13.]

Chapter 13

Prayer Burdens

As intercessors, an important part of our role is knowing how to recognize and respond to prayer burdens for our children. If we are paying attention, it is often easy to discern when our children are struggling. The Bible tells us "out of the abundance of the heart the mouth speaks." So, just by listening to what they communicate to us or their friends, we are able to identify their struggle or need (Luke 6:46). These struggles become a target of our prayers. However, at times the struggle will be hidden beneath the surface or related to an attack against our children we cannot yet see in the natural. At these times, the Holy Spirit wants to prophetically alert us of the need so we can intercede before we see the need for it in the natural. I call this sort of alert a prayer burden.

Many times, we do not know why the burden has come, but the Spirit knows, and we can trust Him to guide us in our prayers so we can release protection over our children in the spirit. Jesus promised that "the Spirit of truth" would "guide you into all the truth" and "tell you what is yet to come" (John 16:13). God wants to give us the inside scoop on what's happening with our kids so that we can pray on their behalf.

One night, when Danielle was about ten years old, I went into her bedroom to say goodnight and to pray over her. When I put my hand on her shoulder, I saw in my spirit what looked like darts coming to her mind. I knew these were fiery darts or thoughts from the enemy (see Ephesians 6:16), but I didn't know what the thoughts were. Looking back, I now realize this warfare was a plot of the enemy to build a stronghold in her life. I wish I had done more to address this warfare by teaching her how to resist the lies and by specifically interceding against what I saw. The warfare lasted about ten years.

One day, after Danielle graduated from college, she told me what the warfare was. I was annoyed with myself that I hadn't been more aggressive in dealing with it, especially since God had given me this prayer burden on her behalf. Yet, God redeemed the years of struggle in her life, and she had a major encounter with God when she was praying alone in her apartment. Afterward, she told me, "Mommy, I was instantly set free, and I have never been bombarded with those lies anymore."

At another time, I was in my office praying for what I saw coming for future ministry, which included travel. I was praying for open doors and that God would go before me and prepare the way. While I was praying, I had a vision of my daughter Jaclyn sitting in her canopy bed praying. I heard the Lord say to me, "There is another kind of praying going on in this house. She is praying that you won't travel." I was shocked! At that time, God had been speaking to me about a season of relaunch after the kids were older. Jaclyn must have heard me talking about it and thought I was talking about traveling while she was still young.

I will never forget that day. When I saw Jaclyn get off the bus, I knew I had inside information on her! It was as real to me as the car I was sitting in. After giving the kids a snack, I took Jaclyn into my office, and I told her what the Lord had said to me. Immediately, she began to cry and told me all the things she was worried about and how much she needed me to be home. In response, I showed her Proverbs 31:16 which God used to tell me that my family must come first and that I should not accept any speaking engagements that would cause hardship to my family. She was relieved. Through this spiritual alert, God helped me to see an issue in my daughter's heart so I could clear up the misunderstanding and prevent any breakdown in our relationship.

Spiritual Prayer Alerts

Spiritual prayer alerts can come to us in a variety of ways. The more we pay attention to the still small voice of God, the more likely we will be to catch these alerts and engage in prayer. In my experience, prayer alerts most often come in one of the following ways.

1. **An Inner Knowing:** The primary way God speaks to us is through an inner knowing. We just know in our hearts that something isn't right with one of our children. It isn't rooted in fear, but is a consistent steady knowing.
2. **An Inner Witness:** An inner witness is similar to a knowing in our hearts, but the inner witness is more like a sudden alert on the inside. For example, one day as I walked through my foyer, I happened to look at a picture of one of my children. At that moment, my spirit jumped, and I felt an alert that something wasn't right with her.
3. **A Word of Knowledge:** A word of knowledge, a word of wisdom, and discerning of spirits are revelation gifts mentioned in the Bible (see 1 Corinthians 12:7–10). These gifts manifest as the Spirit wills, but as praying parents, we should covet them. A Word of Knowledge reveals something within the realm of knowledge—facts, events (past or present), purpose, motive, origin, or destiny. The information can be human, divine, or satanic; it can be natural or supernatural.

    When we receive a word of knowledge, we receive information about something in the past or present we do not have any way of knowing in the natural. It is a supernatural revelation by the Spirit. He gives us information from the mind of God about a person, place, or thing.

4. **A Word of Wisdom:** A word of wisdom is similar to a word of knowledge except it pertains to the future. It is a supernatural revelation by the Spirit of God concerning the plan and purpose in the mind of God.

5. **A Discerning of Spirits:** To discern means to see. Discerning of spirits gives us insight into the spirit realm. As praying parents, this gift helps us to know if evil spirits are trying to influence our children—versus something arising from their souls. This gift also gives us insight into thoughts and intents of the heart, as well as motives. This gift is helpful to parents in many ways. It can even help us discern whether our kids' friends are good for them.

6. **A Scripture:** The Holy Spirit can communicate a prayer burden to us through a passage of Scripture. God's Word is living and active, and the Spirit can use it to enlighten us about particular situations. I experienced this one night when I went into Danielle's bedroom for our regular nighttime prayer. Suddenly, Mathew 6:25–34 rose up from my heart into my mind. These verses talk about anxiety and worry. Danielle was very young at the time, and I was surprised that even at her age she would be wrestling with this in her soul. I said to her, "Do you worry?" Shocked, she looked up at me with her big eyes and nodded. I told her God loves her so much and that He had just told me He did not want her to worry about things. I was able to not only pray with her, but to spend time teaching her how to give her worries to God.

7. **A Vision or Dream:** Sometimes we receive prayer alerts through dreams or visions (see Job 33:14–15).

8. **A Heaviness of Spirit:** At times, God clues us into a prayer need through a heaviness in our spirits or a feeling of being grieved in our spirits. It can be slight, or it can be heavy. It is intended as an alarm on the inside. This is like a pain on the inside, but not in the physical realm. It comes from our spirits by the Holy Spirit, and it can be felt in our souls and sometimes manifest in our bodies. When we think about certain people, something on the inside is grieved or pained (see Acts 16:18). This is a sign that it is time to pray.
9. **A Strong Love:** Finally, we can receive a prayer alert when a stronger than usual love rises up from within our hearts for one particular child (see Romans 5:5). This love transcends our human love and is a manifestation of God's love for that child (see Matthew 7:11). This *agape* love will especially manifest when there is a need for a deeper level of prayer, like travail.

Pause and Reflect…

Review the descriptions and determine to be more aware of these alerts as you pray for your child.

These are some of the more common ways that we can receive prayer alerts for our children, though God is not limited by these. The key is that we are tuned in to the Spirit so we can hear Him when He signals the need for extra prayer. Paul says, "For those who are led by the Spirit of God are the children of God" (Romans 8:14). We are His children, and our children are His as well. He wants to lead us as intercessors for our children so they can grow and thrive in Him. When we pay attention to these prayer alerts, not only can we release blessings and breakthroughs in their lives, but we can also abort the plans of the enemy against them.

A friend told me the story of her youngest son and how she responded to a prayer alert she received during a difficult time in his life. He struggled with low self-esteem and depression in high school because of bullying and the loss of a close relationship with his father after his father had an affair and his parents got divorced. Her son took it very hard, but he gave his heart to the Lord, and God was with him. After graduating from high school, he went to college, where he met a girl he adored and hoped to eventually marry. He also excelled academically, athletically, and musically, and received a significant award and scholarship. All seemed to be going well for him.

However, when my friend met his girlfriend, she felt God speak clearly to her, telling her the relationship would not last, his heart would be broken, and he would have difficulty recovering. My friend had always prayed God would send incredible women for her sons and that she would recognize them when they arrived. This word from God was not what she expected or wanted to hear, but she immediately made it a matter of prayer.

A year later, her son's girlfriend did break up with him and revealed that she had been involved with someone else while dating him. He was devastated. The feelings of betrayal and rejection were so strong that he dropped out of school. To cope with the pain, he began smoking marijuana day and night. He had lost his scholarship at school, so he was struggling financially. When some new friends showed him how to deal drugs, he saw it as the answer to his need for money. Before long, he had become one of the biggest drug dealers in the area.

One day, while his mother was on her way to the store, she began to feel a strong prayer burden to pray for him. She also received a word of knowledge that he was in trouble, and she needed to pray immediately. She began to pray in tongues and could feel the depth of the urgency by the Spirit and how the Spirit was praying through her. She felt as though she was fighting for his life. After about a half-hour, the burden lifted, and she thanked God that no weapon formed against her son would prosper. She also felt led to pray that any relationships in his life that were not ordained by God would end. She prayed that the plans God had for his life would not be thwarted by the enemy.

A few months later, everything began to come into the light in her son's life. He was arrested for dealing drugs and ended up in prison for thirty days. Yet, through that experience, God met him and turned his life around. He rededicated his life to God in prison and also broke free of his addiction to marijuana. When he got out, he became active in church again, and it wasn't long before he met the woman who would eventually become his wife. To this day, they are still married and serving God in ministry together.

My friend believes the radical shift that happened in his life was birthed that day when God put a prayer burden in her heart. Though she didn't know what was going on or what would happen, she was obedient to pray according to the Spirit's leading. Though initially her son's circumstances seemed to get worse when he landed in jail, it was actually the open door he needed to lead him back to his relationship with God. As this story shows us, recognizing and responding to prayer alerts is an important part of effectively interceding for our children.

When we pray the prayer of intercession for our children, we partner with God in bringing Heaven to earth in their lives. He loves it when we intercede for our kids because our prayers reflect His heart. God loves it when we come to Him expecting exceedingly and abundantly above and beyond all we can ask, hope, dream, or think (see Ephesians 3:20). He is love, and He cannot fail. Moreover, He has given us our children as a reward and heritage. He wants them to thrive even more than we do. He is a wonderful friend to us, and we can always come to Him for help. He promises to give us the victory!

> *But thanks be to God! He gives us the victory through our Lord Jesus Christ. Therefore, my dear brothers and sisters, stand firm. Let nothing move you. Always give yourselves*

fully to the work of the Lord, because you know that your labor in the Lord is not in vain. (1 Corinthians 15:57–58)

The victory is assured when we remain steadfast and unmovable laborers in intercession. Our prayers for our children will not be in vain. Eventually, we will reap the reward for our perseverance and faith, and we will see our children walking with the Lord (see 3 John 1:4).

Digging Deeper Workbook Chapters 12 and 13

Read Job 22:27-30.

You will pray to Him, and He will hear you, and you will pay your vows. You will also decide and decree a thing, and it will be established for you; and the light [of God's favor] will shine upon your ways. When you are cast down and humbled, you will speak with confidence, and the humble person He will lift up and save. He will even rescue the one [for whom you intercede] who is not innocent; and he will be rescued through the cleanness of your hands. (Job 22:27–30 AMP)

Define the prayer of intercession:

Define the word *importunity*

Review these Powerful Parenting Insights:

Powerful Parenting Insights

- When we stand in the gap for our children, we are releasing the ministry of Jesus and agreeing with what God has already said about their destiny.
- When we do this, in the spirit we are laying one hand on them and one hand on God.
- As we continue steadfastly, unmovable in persistent intercession, we are pulling our children out of spiritual darkness and toward the Kingdom of light.

Review these power insights concerning the importance of interceding for our children:

- As an intercessor, we can spiritually take a stand in that broken place and forbid the enemy from entering.
- When we intercede for our children, we are setting in motion the will of God in their lives.
- When we connect our natural love to the supernatural grace of God in intercession, we will have the strength to persevere in prayer until a breakthrough comes.
- Intercession involves persisting in prayer for another person *until* the breakthrough comes (see Luke 18:1).

Read, Memorize, and Daily Declare Hebrews 4:12.

For the word of God is alive and active. Sharper than any double-edged sword, it penetrates even to dividing soul and spirit, joints and marrow; it judges the thoughts and attitudes of the heart. (Hebrews 4:12)

Pray

Father God, thank You that Your Word is quick and powerful and sharper than any two-edged sword, separating spirit and soul. I bind any soul control and release the sword of Your Word to cut that control of any unhealthy relationships and soul ties that are preventing my child from being free to pursue Your plan for their life. Help me to be more aware of Your spiritual prayer alerts and immediately respond as Your Spirit directs.

Chapter 14

The Warrior

As we intercede for our children in prayer, there will be times when we also need to engage in spiritual warfare to get the breakthrough we are seeking. Simply defined, spiritual warfare is using our authority to rebuke the enemy and command him to leave our children alone. As a general rule, it is important to remember our focus must always be on God and what He is doing. The Bible makes it clear that the devil is our enemy, intent on attacking us, and it is important to know how to war in the spirit. The Bible tells us, "Be alert and of sober mind. Your enemy the devil prowls around like a roaring lion looking for someone to devour. Resist him, standing firm in the faith" (1 Peter 5:8–9). God clearly tells us we must not ignore the devil and the influence he can have on our children's lives. Instead, we must resist him.

Our children do experience spiritual warfare at times, therefore, we must take authority over demonic influences in their lives, whether they are believers or unbelievers. Though believers cannot be possessed by demons, they can be oppressed. This can happen for a variety of reasons. Sin, self-pity, unforgiveness, bitterness, hatred, fear, deception, and the like can all open doors for demonic activity in believers' lives. Sometimes, believers may experience oppression simply because they are weak in their faith or because they are worn out and tired—physically, emotionally, mentally, or spiritually—and need additional prayer support. Also, if a child was victimized or abused, that trauma can open a door for demonic activity.

If our children do not yet believe in Jesus, the Bible tells us they are under the influence of the devil, and they are blind to the truth of Christ (see 2 Corinthians 4:4). They have been walking according to the course of this world, under the influence of the prince of the power of the air, the spirit who now works in the children of disobedience (see Ephesians 2:2). Because of this, we must step in and take authority in the spirit on their behalf, removing the veil over their eyes so they can see and receive Jesus for who He is.

Freeing the Captives

Paul talks in the most detail about spiritual warfare in Ephesians 6. He tells us our battle is not against people, but against spirits of darkness that want to abort the plan of God. Although people often commit evil under the influence of demons, the people are never our enemies. Our true enemy is the forces of spiritual darkness (see Ephesians 6:10–12). After clarifying who our enemy is, Paul describes the armor we need to effectively fight that enemy:

> *Therefore put on the full armor of God, so that when the day of evil comes, you may be able to stand your ground, and after you have done everything, to stand. Stand firm then, with the **belt of truth** buckled around your waist, with the **breastplate of righteousness** in place, and with your **feet fitted with the readiness** that comes from the gospel of peace. In addition to all this, take up the **shield of faith**, with which you can extinguish all the flaming arrows of the evil one. Take the **helmet of salvation** and the **sword of the Spirit**, which is the word of God.* (Ephesians 6:13–17 emphasis added)

Paul tells us we have everything we need to be effective intercessors and warriors for our families. Each one of us received this armor when we received Jesus into our lives. Though we have an enemy, we have the greater One within us, and our victory is assured. "You, dear children, are from God and have overcome them, because the one who is in you is greater than the one who is in the world" (1 John 4:4). We are filled with the Spirit of Christ, and He has commissioned us with spiritual power to overcome the enemy (see Matthew 28:18–20; Mark 16:17).

During His life on earth, Jesus went about doing good and freeing those who were oppressed by the devil (see Acts 10:38). Then, shortly before His death, He told His disciples, "Very truly I tell you, whoever believes in me will do the works I have been doing, and they will do even greater things than these, because I am going to the Father" (John 14:12).

> **Jesus has called us to bring freedom to the captives. He has given us the authority of His name to do it. We have been recruited into the heavenly police force, and Jesus' name is our badge, our proof of power.**

Powerful Parenting Insights

- We can take authority over the devil and command him to release his hold on our children in Jesus' name.
- In Jesus' name, we can bind all demonic influences—all sorcery, witchcraft, word curses, palm reading, and the like—and declare them of no effect in our children's lives.
- We can also break generational curses over a family line and release freedom in Jesus' name.
- We can quench the fiery darts of the enemy, the lies that seek to bring oppression, depression, and suicidal thoughts

into our children's minds. All these must bow and flee at the name of Jesus!

Every circumstance our children face is different, but the solution is always the same. As parental intercessors, we can use the name of Jesus and free our children from demonic strongholds. We have that authority. However, before we start rebuking a demon at every corner, we need to get a holistic picture of our children and learn to discern the source of their struggles. God wants us to spiritually discern the root of the issues our kids face—whether they come from a spiritual attack or from an issue with their soul or body. Then we will know how to properly deal with the issue.

The Need for Discernment

I believe the root cause of much of the oppression our children experience is a spiritual attack. However, not everything bad that happens is from the devil. Some of the things our children go through are just a natural part of development in their souls (mind, will, and emotions). Even their bodies can cause struggle. Changing hormones, chemical imbalances, improper diet, and food allergies can have a real effect on their moods. Like us, our children came from the heart of God (see Jeremiah 1:5). Each one of us is a spirit, who has a soul, and lives in a body (see 1 Thessalonians 5:23). Though our spirits are meant to be the dominant part of our person, the soul and body are also important and can be the source of struggle if they are not properly cared for.

This is especially true in the souls of our children, as they undergo the many changes and experience the social pressures of the pre-teen and teen years. Our children can have areas of struggle in their souls that are not an issue of spiritual warfare. If they have a tendency toward weakness in an area of their souls, the enemy will try to take advantage of them in that area. He will try to turn it into an issue of warfare. As parents, we must be aware of this and be sensitive to any open doors for the devil. It is also helpful to know what personalities our children have because certain personalities are more susceptible to certain kinds of warfare. Warfare that affects one child may have no impact on another, depending on their temperament or personality type.

When we know what is really going on with our kids, then we will know how to address it. One of the best ways we can do this is to know each of our children well, to know their personalities and their strengths and weaknesses. This will help us know the areas where they may be more susceptible to attack. When my children were small, I decided to have complete personality profiles done on them so I could more effectively parent them according to their temperament.[51] I also read *The 5 Love Languages of our Children* by Gary Chapman and Ross Campbell to learn more about what makes my kids feel loved and understood.

Knowledge is power. This knowledge helped me tremendously in how I parent my children. It also gave me insight into what areas might be most susceptible to attack and how to intercede for my children.

Pause and Reflect…

> *God has given each of your children certain love languages and their own unique temperament to go along with their spiritual gifts and destiny.*
>
> *What have you discovered about your child's love language and unique temperament?*

The enemy doesn't know everything. He is not a mind-reader, but he has been around long enough that he is able to read personalities in people. He is good at discerning the call on people's lives, and then he does everything he can to undermine and attack that destiny and the gifts God has placed within them. This is not just true of adults, but also of children. The enemy is terrified of what they might become if they step into their destiny, so he is working extra hard to distract or deceive them. He has heard all the incredible prophetic words over the rising generations. He knows they are destined to be is his worst nightmare, and he will do all he can to stop them.

For example, if a child has a strong leadership gift, the enemy may try to plant seeds of rebellion or pride. For those who have a strong-willed child, I recommend the books *Raising the New Strong-Willed Child* and *Parenting the Strong-Willed Child* by Dr. James Dobson. These books helped me tremendously because strong-willed children need to be parented in a way that does not break their spirits. If we break their spirits, we break the gift God has put within them. God created them as born leaders, but of course, they are not ready to lead us when they are three years old!

Another example is a very sensitive child who may have a prophetic call. Sensitive children are more prone to being quiet and introverted. For this reason, the enemy often tries to take advantage of them at night when they are alone. This kind of child may not always share what they are thinking unless we spend quality time alone with them and create a safe space for them to share. They may be prone to becoming introspective, depressed, and lonely because they discern what is going on in others, but often don't know how to separate what they discern from their own emotions. With children like these, we need to intentionally draw them out and check in on how they're feeling about life. It can be easy to miss the signs of struggle because their world is more internal than some other children's.

For this reason, when I raised my kids, I tried to always sit with each one alone before they went to sleep. I would sit and talk with them and then lay hands on them and pray over them. Even when they had sleepovers with their friends at our house, I would ask if it was okay if I prayed with them and their friends. So often, by the time it reached the kids' bedtime, I was already completely exhausted from the day's activities, but I intentionally made this a habit. I reminded myself that one day they would be older, and I needed to cherish every moment and seize the opportunity to lay hands on them in prayer while they were in my home. Not only that, but all my prayers are eternal, and long after I leave this earth, my prayers for my children will continue to produce fruit in their lives.

Powerful Parenting Insights

> ➤ **Knowing about our kids and paying attention to what is going on with them spiritually, emotionally, mentally, and physically will help us greatly in our prayers and warfare.**
> ➤ **When we can discern the source of the problem, then we will know how to pray and whether warfare is needed.**

In the following pages, I will highlight two strategies for warring in the spirit for our children—removing spiritual weights and defeating the enemy's lies. While these two ideas overlap, I find it helpful to distinguish between them.

Removing the Weights

Our first strategy in spiritual warfare is removing spiritual weights from our children. We are all in a spiritual race, including our children (see Hebrews 12:1–2). At times, our children may pick up weights that slow them down and keep them from running successfully. These weights can be the result of sin, wounds from other people, or even weariness. These burdens can cause our children to stumble and fall, and some may have a hard time getting back up. In these times, our kids need a revelation of the love of God, as well as strength in their inner person so they can rise up in victory (see Romans 8:37). Through the prayer of intercession, we can lift the weights from their shoulders in the spirit. Instead of becoming fearful when we see our children struggling, we must put on our armor and go to battle on their behalf.

Paul talked about this when he said, "We who are strong ought to bear with the failings of the weak and not to please ourselves" (Romans 15:1) and "Carry each other's burdens, and in this way you will fulfill the law of Christ" (Galatians 6:2). In Romans 5:1, the word Paul uses for *failings* refers to a wrong belief, not a physical weakness. When we bear or carry our children's burdens, we don't take those burdens upon ourselves, but we lift them up to Christ. We do this by partnering with the Holy Spirit and praying according to Romans 8:26–28, where it says we intercede with "wordless groans." My spirit, by the Holy Spirit, will remove burdens from our shoulders and carry them away. Through intercession on behalf of our children, we can partner with Christ's saving power and help free our kids to live a successful Christian life.

When we intercede to lift the weights from our children, we lay one hand on them and one hand on God. As we pray in the spirit, we are lifting off wrong mindsets. We are lifting off the darkness and the lies. We are lifting off all negative thinking that has kept them bound and blind to God's call on their lives.

> *...that the God of our Lord Jesus Christ, the Father of glory, may give to you the spirit of wisdom and revelation in the knowledge of Him, the eyes of your understanding being enlightened; that you may know what is the hope of His calling, what are the riches of the glory of His inheritance in the saints, and what is the exceeding greatness of His power toward us who believe, according to the working of His mighty power.* (Ephesians 1:17-19 NKJV)

As we pray Ephesians 1:17-19 over them, we release a revelation of God's love to their hearts and minds which releases a supernatural strength and grace to overcome. One of my favorite strategies is to insert the name of the person I'm praying for into Hebrews 12:1-2, declare it aloud, and then pray in tongues.

> *Therefore, since you, _____ (insert name), are surrounded by such a great cloud of witnesses, throw off everything that hinders and the sin that so easily entangles. Run with perseverance the race marked out for you, fixing your eyes on Jesus, the pioneer and perfecter of faith. For the joy set before Him, He endured the cross, scorning its shame, and sat down at the right hand of the throne of God.*

Sometimes, when I have prayed like this, the battle has been so intense that I have literally felt a tug of war in my spirit. In these moments, it is time to persist fervently until I receive a note of victory, or what I call a release in the spirit. This is a signal from the Holy Spirit that the victory has been accomplished in prayer.

Defeating the Lies

The second strategy in warfare is defeating the lies the enemy whispers to our children. Often, spiritual warfare comes against our children in the shape of lies that enter their minds. The devil is a liar, and the primary way he attacks believers is through whispering lies into our ears and hoping we will believe them. The Bible refers to these lies as "flaming arrows" (Ephesians 6:16). If we do not shoot them down, they can begin an insidious attack against our faith in God and our identity in Him. Kids often do not know how to recognize when the enemy lies to them, and they assume that every thought that comes into their minds is their own.

Too often, our children are not aware enough to know how to rebuke him on their own, and they need us to fight for them. In Isaiah 54, God promises good things for our children—including freedom from attack and oppression.

> *All your children will be taught by the LORD, and great will be their peace. In righteousness you will be established: tyranny will be far from you; you will have nothing to fear. Terror will be far removed; it will not come near you. If anyone does attack you, it will not be my doing; whoever attacks you will surrender to you…no weapon forged against you will prevail, and you will refute every tongue that accuses you. This is the heritage of the servants of the LORD, and this is their vindication from me.* (Isaiah 54:13–17)

When we see our children are believing lies about themselves or about God, it is time to stand up and fight on their behalf. It is time to declare that no weapon will prosper against them and that their minds will be free from oppression. The apostle Paul tells us exactly how to do this in Ephesians 6, where he talks in detail about spiritual warfare. He says, "Take up the shield of faith, with which you can extinguish all the flaming arrows of the evil one" (Ephesians 6:16). The perfect weapon against the enemy's lies is unyielding faith in God's promises. Through faith, we step into our authority as believers, and we can command the enemy to be silent and to leave our children alone. Through faith, we declare the truth of God that counters the enemy's lies, just as Jesus did when Satan tempted Him in the wilderness (see Matthew 4:1–11).

When we command him to be silent, the devil must obey.

Living in Freedom

The goal of spiritual warfare is freedom for spiritual captives. Weights are removed. Lies are silenced and our children are free to walk with God. This is what the gospel is all about. Of course, spiritual warfare is an ongoing battle in all our lives, but I believe we can see measurable breakthrough that frees our children to rise above the devil's attack. I also believe it is very important to teach our kids, once they have received Jesus into their hearts, how to recognize the voice of the enemy and how to rebuke him. Children have just as much authority in the spirit as adults, and sometimes they have a lot more faith. They simply need instruction.

If we teach our children how to fight, and then we fight alongside them, we will be equipping them to live free of oppression.

A friend recently told me a story that illustrates both the power of our waring prayers and the power of training our children in spiritual warfare. Several years ago, my friend's family experienced a very devastating time when her daughter and son-in-law lost a child to death. In the wake of this horrible loss, the enemy sought to drive her daughter and son-in-law apart. The two were constantly fighting, even in front of their two young children, and the husband began seeking solace with other women. It wasn't long until they began to talk about separation and divorce.

My friend knew she could not just stand by and watch the devil separate two people who loved God and each other. She began to seek the Lord and pray on their behalf, and the Holy Spirit gave her a word for her daughter. Although her daughter was rightfully angry, my friend called her to see a higher truth—that the enemy was attacking her marriage and she needed to fight to save it. She listened.

She began listening to various Christian programs for marriage, and she made a prayer room and began fighting for her marriage in the spirit. Every time she felt like she wanted to argue with her husband about something, she would remind herself that Satan is the accuser of the brethren and that he was lying to her about her husband. She also reminded herself that God wanted to heal her marriage. My friend and her husband also prayed. They counseled their daughter to speak into existence what she wanted to see in her marriage. They began to call her husband a man after God's own heart, saying that he was a great husband and father.

As my friend's daughter took this stance in prayer, backed by her parents, they began to see real change in their marriage. Her husband agreed to start going with the family to church, and he attended several marriage events with her. His attitudes also began to change, and he started telling her that he loves his life with her. He also began coming home on time and doing things with the family again. In a fairly short time, they went from being on the brink of divorce to learning how to heal and have a healthy marriage. The entire family is once again happy. What the devil meant for their harm, God used to bring them closer to one another and to Him.

Not long ago, my friend's daughter called her to ask if the devil would continue to attack her marriage. My friend told her yes—that he will attack not only her marriage, but everything she holds dear, because his mission is to steal, kill, and destroy (see John 10:10), but because she has God on her side, she has the victory. This is the truth we can cling to. When we fight for our children in the spirit, we will see results. The enemy must bow to the will of God for their lives when we, as praying parents, stand firm and command the enemy to leave.

When we fulfill our call as intercessory warriors, standing guard over our children in the spirit, what we accomplish will be incredible. The impact of our prayers will be far greater than we can imagine.

Digging Deeper Workbook Chapter 14

Read Isaiah 54:13-17 and Reflect on the highlighted words and phrases.

> *All your children will be taught by the* LORD, *and* **great will be their peace.** *In righteousness you will be established: tyranny will be far from you;* **you will have nothing to fear.** *Terror will be far removed; it will not come near you. If anyone does attack you, it will not be my doing; whoever attacks you will surrender to you…**no weapon forged against you will prevail**, and you will refute every tongue that accuses you. This is the heritage of the servants of the* LORD, *and this is their vindication from me.*

Explain the goal of spiritual warfare:

Declare these Powerful Parenting Insights over your children:

- ➤ We can take authority over the devil and command him to release his hold on our children in Jesus' name.
- ➤ In Jesus' name, we can bind all demonic influences—all sorcery, witchcraft, word curses, palm reading, and the like—and declare them of no effect in our children's lives.
- ➤ We can also break generational curses over a family line and release freedom in Jesus' name.

- We can quench the fiery darts of the enemy, the lies that seek to bring oppression, depression, and suicidal thoughts into our children's minds. All these must bow and flee at the name of Jesus!

Review these Powerful Parenting Insights

- Knowing about our kids and paying attention to what is going on with them spiritually, emotionally, mentally, and physically will help us greatly in our prayers and warfare.
- When we can discern the source of the problem, then we will know how to pray and whether warfare is needed.

Keep a journal of what God reveals to you about each child. Write out your specific prayer and describe the warfare you are using over each of them.

Review these power insights concerning the importance of fulfilling your call as an intercessory warrior.

- You have everything you need to be effective intercessors and warriors for your family (see Ephesians 6:13–17).
- Jesus has given you the authority of His name to do it. You have been recruited into the heavenly police force, and Jesus' name is your badge, your proof of power.
- Standing guard over your children in the spirit will accomplish the incredible.
- The impact of your prayers will be far greater than you can imagine.
- When you command him to be silent, the devil must obey.

> If you teach your children how to fight, and then fight alongside them, you will be equipping them to live free of oppression.

Read, Memorize, and Daily Declare these powerful scriptures over each of your children:

> [Jesus said,] "Very truly I tell you, whoever believes in me will do the works I have been doing, and they will do even greater things than these, because I am going to the Father." (John 14:12)

> "You, dear children, are from God and have overcome them, because the one who is in you is greater than the one who is in the world." (1 John 4:4)

Pray and Declare:

Therefore, since you, _____ (insert name), are surrounded by such a great cloud of witnesses, throw off everything that hinders and the sin that so easily entangles. Run with perseverance the race marked out for you, fixing your eyes on Jesus, the pioneer and perfecter of faith. For the joy set before Him, He endured the cross, scorning its shame, and sat down at the right hand of the throne of God.

Remember: "Be alert and of sober mind. Your enemy the devil prowls around like a roaring lion looking for someone to devour. Resist him, standing firm in the faith." (1 Peter 5:8–9)

God gives each of your children certain love languages and their own unique temperament to go along with their spiritual gifts and destiny.

Do a personality profile on them so you can more effectively parent them according to their temperament.[52]

Read *The 5 Love Languages of our Children* by Gary Chapman and Ross Campbell to learn more about what makes your kids feel loved and understood.

Begin a journal for each of your children and record what you learn and how you have partnered with God to help them run their race and have victory over everything the enemy tries to do in their lives.

Chapter 15

The Three Dimensions of Prayer

I n 1 Corinthians 14:15, the apostle Paul talks about different ways to pray. "I will pray with my spirit, but I will also pray with my understanding; I will sing with my spirit, but I will also sing with my understanding." He's not talking about different types of prayer like the difference between intercession and the prayer of faith. Instead, he's talking about different ways or dimensions we can pray.

There are three main dimensions of prayer mentioned in the Bible:

1. Praying the Bible (the scriptures)
2. Praying in tongues (in the spirit)
3. Travailing or groaning in the Spirit

Praying the Bible

The first dimension of prayer involves praying based on the promises of God from the Bible that apply to our children. When we pray God's promises, we know we are praying in alignment with God's will. This increases our faith because the Bible links praying God's will with receiving what we have prayed for (see 1 John 5:14–15).

When we align ourselves with God's Word, we align ourselves with incredible power. We see this in what the Roman centurion said to Jesus, "Just say the word, and my servant will be healed" (Matthew

8:8). The centurion knew all it took was a word of authority. That is the kind of authority we pray with when we pray the Bible.

The Word of God is not static, but dynamic. It is living and active, and it is capable of penetrating people's hearts and turning them toward God (see Hebrews 4:12). It has the power to penetrate any circumstance, and it will not return void. God says, "So is my word that goes out from my mouth: it will not return to me empty, but will accomplish what I desire and achieve the purpose for which I sent it" (Isaiah 55:11). He told the prophet, Jeremiah, "I am watching to see that my word is fulfilled" (Jeremiah 1:12). We can put our full confidence and assurance in His Word.

God does not lie or go back on His Word (see Numbers 23:19). Paul says, "For no matter how many promises God has made, they are 'Yes' in Christ. And so through him the 'Amen' is spoken by us to the glory of God" (2 Corinthians 1:20). In Christ, we have a guarantee that God's promises to us will come true. By faith, we agree with His promises over our lives even before we see them manifest in the natural. This is what it means to pray the Scriptures.

For example, in John 10:10, Jesus says He came to give us abundant life. When I pray a scripture like this, I declare the promise aloud. "Jesus, You said in Your Word that You came to give my children abundant life." Then, I thank Him for that promise, and I decree it over my children. "Thank You, Jesus, for that promise of abundance in all areas of life. I release that over each of my children in the name of Jesus. I come against anything that is seeking to hinder that abundance, and I open the doors for God's goodness and mercy to flow in their lives." Praying Bible verses like this are both simple and effective.

Powerful Parenting Insights

> ➢ Praying for our child's needs from the Bible helps us to agree with God's solution instead of agreeing with the problem or praying worry prayers.
> ➢ Find a verse or verses that apply to their situation.
> ➢ Then pray and declare them aloud over our children.
> ➢ Put their names directly into the verse and declare it out loud.[53]

It is important that we do not focus our prayers on the problem. Yes, we can acknowledge it, but then we must concentrate our prayer and warfare on the solution. The Bible tells us that as we declare God's truth over a situation, our words create real change.

> *You will also declare a thing, and it will be established for you; so light will shine on your ways.* (Job 22:28 NKJV)

Praying in Tongues

The second dimension of prayer is praying in tongues. This is very different from praying the Bible, which we pray with our understanding. When we pray in tongues, we pray by the Spirit (see 1 Corinthians 14:15). Sometimes, we may feel overwhelmed by what our children are facing, and we do not know how to pray for them. Maybe we are unsure what root issue needs to be addressed or what would be best for our children. When we have prayed all that we know to pray in alignment with God's Word, then it is time to pray by the Spirit, who knows more about our children than we will ever know.

Jesus promised His followers, "You will receive power when the Holy Spirit comes on you" (Acts 1:8). That promise was fulfilled when they were baptized with the Spirit and began to speak in tongues (see

Acts 2:1–4). Since that time, that same power has been available to all believers. We have the Spirit of the Lord living within us just like Jesus did. His wisdom and understanding are released as we pray in tongues to produce abundant prayer fruit in our families, and we lack nothing in prayer. We are empowered with a supernatural prayer language that engages Heaven and lays hold of tremendous possibility. Such prayers will produce miracles.

Not long ago, I had a dream about my daughter, Jaclyn. In the dream, we were trying to get into her car, but the car was locked. I said, "Jaclyn, we are locked out. Do you have a key?" She did not have the key. Symbolically, a car represents a person's vocation or ministry. I knew God gave me that dream because I needed to pray for Jaclyn. In the natural, I had, at that time moved her to California to pursue her career. I felt good about her decision and blessed her to go. Prior to this dream, the only thing I had heard the Lord say was, "Jaclyn will find her way." In my heart, I knew He was referring to her career.

A few weeks after this dream, I decided to devote a few hours of my morning to pray for her in the Spirit. I prayed out several things in English as well, including any Bible verses that came to mind, but I spent a good amount of the time praying in tongues. After some time, I found myself speaking out the word *opportunity*. I kept praying in tongues, and several more times, that same word came out of my mouth.

When I told Jaclyn about the prayer assignment and word I received for her, she asked whether I thought it was an opportunity that would happen soon. I told her I didn't know, but that I was confident God was working on her behalf to bring her the success she desired. I also instructed her, as a mentor would, to bring some areas into alignment to position herself to receive God's best. A few months later, I went to visit her. I was amazed to discover that even though she had only been in California for a year, she had made many contacts (divine appointments) that have contributed to her career. I believe her hard work and my time of praying in tongues in response to the dream opened the door in the spirit for Jaclyn to have increased opportunity and open doors to help her thrive in her career.

The ability to pray in tongues is an incredible gift to us. When we pray in tongues, the Spirit prays with knowledge of the deepest mysteries about our children. No matter how well we know our children, their stories still contain many unknowns for us. Only God knows them and their destiny perfectly. Only He knows how to draw it forth (see Ecclesiastes 3:11; Jeremiah 1:5). Empowering us to pray is one of the Holy Spirit's main functions in our lives.

> *In the same way, the Spirit helps us in our weaknesses. We do not know what we ought to pray for, but the Spirit himself intercedes for us through wordless groans. And he who searches our hearts knows the mind of the Spirit, because the Spirit intercedes for God's people in accordance with the will of God. And we know that in all things God works for the good of those who love him, who have been called according to his purpose.* (Romans 8:26–28)

We have an indwelling intercessor. He longs for us to be open channels through whom He can release His powerful ministry. He is a great help in our weakness. Arthur Wallis, the author of *Pray in the Spirit*, provides helpful insight on the meaning of the Greek word translated as *help* in Romans 8:26:

> "The word 'help' used here is the translation of one of those fascinating compound verbs so difficult to convey adequately in English. It is found in only one other passage, Luke 10:40, where Martha complains to the Lord about her sister leaving her to do all the work: 'tell her then to *help* me.' Primarily this word means 'to take hold of', but it has a double prefix, meaning 'together with'

and 'instead of'. This may seem at first a contraction in terms, to say that the Spirit takes hold of (our weakness), together with, instead of.' We have in fact a marvelous truth, not merely that the Spirit intervenes in our weakness, but that He does so 'together with' us—for He requires our willing cooperation—and 'instead of' us, for He does for us what we could never so ourselves."[54]

The Spirit of God flowing through us in prayer makes up for our deficiencies. When we don't know how to pray according to the will of God, the Spirit of God helps us. He knows what is best, and with His help, we can pray perfect prayers for our kids. The love God has for our children is even greater than our own, and His love never fails. Romans 8 promises us God works all things together for the good of our children.

Powerful Parenting Insights

- ➤ When we pray for our children by the Spirit, we release good into their lives.
- ➤ The Spirit has perfect knowledge of God's will, and He prays through us accordingly.
- ➤ When we pray in tongues, we are praying the destiny that was in the heart of the Father before He formed them in the womb.
- ➤ The Spirit enables us to pray the exact prayer that will produce Heaven's results.
- ➤ The Spirit gives our prayers perfect aim.

A dear friend of mine recently found out about the fruit of her prayers in tongues for her son. When her son was a young teenager, one night God woke her up in the middle of the night and prompted her to go pray for her son in his room. She went and laid on the floor of his room and prayed in the Spirit. While she prayed, she thought she smelled alcohol, but she didn't know what to make of it because her son was asleep in his bed. Years later, her son told her he had sneaked out of the house earlier that night, taken their car, drove to someone's house, and drank alcohol. She had been completely unaware, but God was not. He woke her up to pray in tongues, and her prayers helped close a destructive door in her son's life.

Even when we have no idea what we are praying for our children, our prayers in the Spirit release Heaven's warfare on their behalf.

Paul said, "If I pray in a tongue, my spirit prays, but my mind is unfruitful" (1 Corinthians 14:14). When we pray in tongues, we won't understand what we are praying, but by faith, we can know that it is the perfect will of God. This may be hard for some to accept, but we don't need to understand everything. We just need to believe what God says is true.

To pray in tongues, we must be willing to yield our control, understanding, and trust in God's wisdom to work through us in ways we don't understand. As Solomon says, "Trust in the Lord with all your heart and lean not on your own understanding; in all your ways submit to him, and he will make your paths straight" (Proverbs 3:5–6). Faith and trust align us with the Father's will.

This is important because the mysterious aspect of tongues has a powerful purpose. When we pray in tongues, we are speaking in the language of Heaven, and only God understands us. "For anyone who speaks in a tongue does not speak to people but to God. Indeed, no one understands them; they utter mysteries by the Spirit" (1 Corinthians 14:2). This makes praying in the spirit a tremendous weapon against any darkness in our children's lives. The enemy hates it when we pray in tongues because he cannot understand what we are saying.

Not only are our prayers perfectly on target, when we pray in the Spirit, the devil remains ignorant of God's strategies.

Arthur Wallis says, "The Holy Spirit needs us to accomplish His intercessory ministry, and we certainly need Him to accomplish ours. What a privilege to be invited to join in a heavenly partnership. He wants to be free to think through our minds, feel through our hearts, speak through our lips and even weep through our eyes and groan through our spirits. When a believer is thus at the disposal of the Holy Spirit, praying in the Spirit will be a reality."[55]

When we pray in the Spirit, we enter into a dynamic and supernatural partnership with God. We allow His words to come out of our mouths. We become His voice on the earth. If we really understand this, we will devote an increasing amount of time to praying in the Spirit. We will follow Paul's advice: "Pray in the Spirit on all occasions with all kinds of prayers and requests. With this in mind, be alert and always keep on praying for all the Lord's people" (Ephesians 6:18). Paul knew the power of praying in tongues, and he did it so much that he could say, "I thank God that I speak in tongues more than all of you" (1 Corinthians 14:18). May we emulate him in our dedication to lending our mouths to the Spirit of the Lord and fanning into flame the gift of God within us (see 2 Timothy 1:6).

I have spent countless hours praying first the Word of God for my children and then praying in the Spirit. Life is not always easy, and raising children comes with many challenges. Thankfully, we are not alone in raising our children into their destinies. We have the Spirit as our great Helper, and His prayers through us are powerful. Praying in tongues is an essential part of intercession, just like praying the Scripture. We must not neglect either of these in our prayers for our children.

Praying with Travail

Romans 8:26 speaks not only of praying in the Spirit, but also specifically of praying through travail when it says, "the Spirit himself intercedes for us through wordless groans." Simply put, travail is a form of intense intercession in our hearts and spirits that can involve deep groanings and tears. It is a spiritual birthing in prayer, and it ends when the intercessor senses a release in the Spirit. Sometimes, this manifests as a sense of breaking or laughter. Unlike the first two dimensions of prayer, travail rises up in our spirits by the Holy Spirit and is always initiated by Him, not by our human will.

In an article for *The Elijah List*, James Goll, a well-known seer, explained travail this way:

> "As it is in the natural, so it is in the spiritual. Travail is a form of intense intercession given by the Holy Spirit whereby an individual or group is gripped by something that grips God's heart. The individual or group labors with Him for an opening to be created so that the new life can come forth.
>
> The definition of travail from *Webster's New World Dictionary* is simple: Noun 1. very hard work. 2. the pains of childbirth. 3. intense pain; agony. Verb- 1. to toil. 2. to suffer the pains of childbirth. I have found this definition describing physical travail to be correct in the spiritual realm as well.

Travail takes place after you have carried something in your heart for a period of time, but it comes on you suddenly. Travail can be associated with the prayer of tears, but does not require it. It is preceded by nurturing the promise; later the strategic time comes to push that promise forth through the prayer canal. Finally, you realize that the promise has been born, and you are greatly relieved when the delivery is over!

The prayer of travail is God desiring to create an "opening" to bring forth a measure of life or growth. If the "opening" was already in place, there would not be the need for travail. Just as the "opening" of the natural womb is enlarged to bring forth the baby, so travail creates an "opening" or "way," whereas before the opening or way was closed. With travail, there is always a way opened for life, newness, change, or growth."[56]

Arthur Wallis adds:

"If some have found the idea of praying in an unknown tongue perplexing, they may find this idea of inarticulate praying even more so, for here there is no language at all—the only speech is signs and the only grammar groans, and even these are silent because inexpressible. It should be emphasized here that this type of praying is not generally for the public gathering but for the secret place. Let us not shut our minds to what at first may appear to be incomprehensible, even irrational. Of course, it is not irrational; like so much else in the realm of the Spirit it is super-rational. Faith can lead us into this realm, but not reason."[57]

Travail is the least "reasonable" dimension of prayer, but it is just as important as the other two dimensions. Of course, we do not always need to go into this dimension of intercession to see results in prayer. We must simply be willing to follow the Spirit's lead and trust that if He takes us into travail that it is necessary in that instance. When the Spirit leads us into travail, it is a manifestation that is accompanied by a greater anointing in prayer. This is because our prayers in travail come straight from our spirits by the Holy Spirit (see John 3:6). In those moments, we have no thought of ourselves, but only a strong desire to bring forth what the Spirit has placed on the inside.

When we enter the place of travail, our hearts and our spirits will be gripped for our children. When I am in travail, I often feel as though my heart is in pain, even to the point of breaking. This happens because at times the Holy Spirit allows us to feel the hearts of the ones we are praying for. We are discerning what is going on in their hearts so we can more effectively and fervently intercede for them.

Sometimes, we feel the heart of God for our children and how He longs for them to be saved, set free, and empowered to live in their destiny. When that happens, we feel a deep yearning and intense love, which is our love as parents combined with the love of the Father for our children. Travail is both emotionally and spiritually intense. Just as childbirth is intense and painful in the natural, so travail can feel very exhausting and emotional, but the struggle is worth it.

Jesus said, "A woman giving birth to a child has pain because her time has come; but when her baby is born she forgets the anguish because of her joy that a child is born into the world" (John 16:21).

Travail is not easy, but it is a great sacrifice of love we can perform for our kids as the Spirit leads. The call to travail in prayer can last for a few hours, or it can last for a more extended time, sometimes for days or even weeks. If we are called into an extended time of travail, we obviously need to continue our daily duties. When this happens, we can simply leave the secret place to go about our day, and then when we can return to the secret place, we just pick up where we left off.

We begin our prayer time with worship, present the one we are praying for before the throne of grace, and begin to pray in tongues. As we yield to the Holy Spirit, He will bring us back into the place of travail. We will know we have finished this prayer assignment when we feel a release on the inside and the sorrow has been replaced with joy or lightness in spirit.

We find an example of travail in Jesus' life in John 11, where Jesus raised Lazarus from the dead. When Mary came to greet Jesus and He saw her grief, "he was deeply moved in spirit and troubled" (John 11:33). Then, after asking where they had laid Lazarus' body, "Jesus wept" (John 11:35). When He came to the tomb, it says He was "once more deeply moved" (John 11:38). The New King James Version says He was "groaning in Himself." After this, Jesus prayed aloud to the Father, thanking Him for always hearing His prayers. Then, He commanded Lazarus to come forth, and Lazarus came back to life and walked out of the tomb. Finally, Jesus told the onlookers to free Lazarus from the grave clothes that were still wrapped around him.

What is interesting about this story is that Jesus thanks the Father for always hearing His prayers, but we do not hear Him pray to ask the Father to raise Lazarus from the dead. This is because when Jesus was deeply moved and troubled in His spirit and then wept, He was travailing in prayer for Lazarus. This was the prayer He referred to when He thanked the Father for hearing Him. Though travail looks and sounds strange to our human ears, the Father understands it, and He answers. After the travail was over, Jesus commanded life back into Lazarus, and he immediately rose from the dead. When Lazarus came out of the tomb, this symbolizes being born again into new creation life (see Ephesians 2:1–2; 2 Corinthians 5:17). When he was freed from his grave clothes, it symbolizes the things that can keep believers bound even after salvation. So, in this story, we see two types of deliverance in response to travail. First, the dead one is birthed back into life. Second, the bound one is birthed into freedom.

When we travail for our children, we are participating in birthing them into the next level of maturity in their spiritual lives. As such, this is a very important aspect of the prayer of intercession and contending for the hearts and destinies of our children. Paul talked about travailing in prayer for his spiritual children so that they would mature in Christ, "My dear children, for whom I am again in the pains of childbirth until Christ is formed in you" (Galatians 4:19). The purpose of travail is specifically to birth our children into a new season or level of maturity so that ultimately Christ will be formed in them.

As we engage in these three dimensions of prayer, we can pray with confidence for our children knowing we are praying in step with the Spirit and will see spiritual fruit manifest in their lives!

Digging Deeper Workbook Chapter 15

Explain the three main dimensions of prayer mentioned in the Bible:

1. Praying the Bible
2. Praying in tongues
3. Travailing or groaning in the Spirit

Read Romans 8:26-28.

In the same way, the Spirit helps us in our weakness. We do not know what we ought to pray for, but the Spirit himself intercedes for us through wordless groans. And he who searches our hearts knows the mind of the Spirit, because the Spirit intercedes for God's people in accordance with the will of God. And we know that in all things God works for the good of those who love him, who have been called according to his purpose. (Romans 8:26–28)

Now Declare these Powerful Parenting Insights over Your children:

- ➤ Even when we have no idea what we are praying for our children, our prayers in the Spirit release Heaven's will on their behalf.
- ➤ Not only are our prayers perfectly on target, when we pray in the Spirit, the devil remains ignorant of God's strategies.
- ➤ As we engage in these three dimensions of prayer, we can pray with confidence for our children knowing we are praying in step with the Spirit and will see spiritual fruit manifest in their lives!

For a more in-depth understanding of these three dimensions of prayer, read and meditate on the key scriptures from this chapter and record what God reveals to you from each one.

1 John 5:14–15
Acts 1:8
Acts 2:1–4
John 3:6

Review these Powerful Parenting Insights

Powerful Parenting Insights

- ➤ Praying for our child's needs from the Bible helps us to agree with God's solution instead of agreeing with the problem.

Have you found you have focused more on the problem than agreeing with God's solution?

- Find a verse or verses that apply to their situation.
- Then pray and declare them aloud over our children.
- Put their names directly into the verse and declare it out loud.[58]
- When we pray for our children in the spirit, we are praying according to the will of God and therefore, can have confidence that He hears us and we have the petitions on the behalf of our children.
- The Spirit has perfect knowledge of God's will, and He prays through us accordingly.
- When we pray in tongues, we are praying into the destiny that was in the heart of the Father before He formed them in the womb.
- The Spirit enables us to pray the exact prayer that will produce Heaven's results.
- The Spirit gives our prayers perfect aim.

Read and Memorize Job 22:28.

The Bible tells us that as we declare God's truth over a situation, our words create real change.

You will also declare a thing, and it will be established for you; so light will shine on your ways." (NKJV)

Pray

Thank You, Father God, for providing me with these three powerful dimensions of prayer so I can be the intercessor warrior my children need me to be for them as they journey forward toward their destiny. I will implement Ephesians 6:18 in my life knowing I am agreeing with Your Word and plan for my children. I will pray in the Spirit on all occasions with all kinds of prayers and requests. I will be alert and always keep on praying for _____ all [Your] people as Your Spirit directs me. When I do not know what to pray, I will surrender my tongue to Your Spirit and ask Him to pray through me for _____.

Chapter 16
Praying with Heaven's Mindset

In the pages of this book, we have talked a lot about why we should pray for our children and effective ways to pray for them. In this final chapter, I want to address how we should respond when we don't immediately see answers to our prayers. We all love to hear the stories of dramatic answers to prayer, but the reality is sometimes we need to persevere in prayer for a season before we see the breakthrough we want. Perseverance is part of the definition of intercession. Jesus taught His disciples "they should always pray and not give up" (Luke 18:1). The same holds true for us, but it is not fun or easy. Sometimes, we may begin to feel discouraged and want to give up. To help us persevere until our prayers are answered, I want to address the three mindsets necessary for success.

The Victory Mindset

> "We do not war *for* victory, as if it were up to our methods and works to obtain it. Rather we war *from* victory. We war *from* a position of intimacy with the Ultimate Victor, and are enforcing the victory He has already purchased." - Bill Johnson, *Hosting the Presence: Unveiling Heaven's Agenda*

The first mindset is the belief that when we engage in spiritual warfare and intercession, we do it **from** victory, not **for** victory. In other words, we know that Jesus has already won the victory for us, and therefore, when we pray, we pray with that mindset. We pray as those who are enforcing the victory of a battle that has already been won, not as those who are trying to gain victory in the first place. The difference may seem subtle, but it deeply impacts the way we subconsciously approach prayer.

In Bill Johnson's workbook, *Hosting the Presence: Unveiling Heaven's Agenda*, he explains this idea well:

> In the Garden, Adam was not given any tools—teaching or training manuals on spiritual warfare. He simply walked in the cool of the day with the Lord. Obviously, the threat of darkness was real and near, as a chaotic world existed just outside of Eden. Satan had now entered the equation. How was mankind expected to subdue darkness and fill the planet with God's government? It was to happen through intimacy.
>
> Kingdom dominion was established through a relationship with the King. Emphasis was not on principles, but on a Person (Jesus). Relationship was prized above all else, for humanity was meant to rule out of relationship and, in turn, exercise authority over darkness out of relationship. When we know who He is, and what life is like in His world, by default the things that conflict and disagree with Him are the very things that must be subdued.
>
> This is not a call to spiritually careless living. Paul admonishes us in 2 Corinthians 2:11 not to be ignorant

of the devil's schemes. Spiritual warfare is a reality that believers need to appropriately engage in. Overemphasis on it, however, is just as unhealthy as ignorance. In the Garden of Eden, satan was not the focus because mankind had not yet sinned and granted him authority. And the same should be true for us—after the Cross, satan should not be the focus. He is a defeated foe.

From the moment mankind fell, God was not taken off guard. Satan is crushed under the feet of man. The Anointed Man, Jesus, won the victory, and ever since His resurrection, anointed men and women throughout the ages have been granted the same position of victory over the serpent. We do not war *for* victory, as if it were up to our methods and works to obtain it. Rather we war *from* victory. We war *from* a position of intimacy with the Ultimate Victor, and are enforcing the victory He has already purchased."[59]

This is a powerful mindset because it changes the way we see God. We are not begging Him to answer our prayers. He has already provided abundant blessings and breakthrough on the cross. Instead, we are agreeing with what He has already ordained and partnering with Him to cause His will to manifest on earth. Also, it changes the way we view the devil. He is not a threatening opponent. He has been forever defeated by Jesus, and we now have authority over him. These truths will help us to keep our hearts right as we persevere in prayer. When it feels like an answer is long in coming, we can know it is not because God is holding out on us. He is not at fault. This keeps us from allowing offense toward Him to grow in our hearts. It also helps us see the big picture of the spiritual battle we are fighting, in which we are subduing insubordinate demons and causing them to submit to the authority of Christ.

The Hope Mindset

The second mindset necessary to perseverance in prayer is the mindset of hope. Discouragement is the number one reason people experience defeat in prayer. They allow hopelessness to slip in, and they stop praying. As a result, they do not see the breakthrough they need. Hope is what keeps us from losing heart and giving up. Steve Backlund, from Bethel Church, defines *hope* as "the confident, joyful expectation good is coming."[60]

> **We could say hope is the overarching belief that we can expect good things to happen in our lives. It is a relentless optimism based on the goodness of God, regardless of our circumstances.**

This may sound undoable to some, but God has called us to live in hope (see Ephesians 1:18). The Bible tells us love "always hopes" (1 Corinthians 13:7). God is never hopeless about our children or the situations they face, and He doesn't want us to be either.

Paul prayed for the early believers, "May the God of hope fill you with all joy and peace as you trust in him, so that you may overflow with hope by the power of the Holy Spirit" (Romans 15:13). God is the God of all hope. He sees it all, yet He is eternally and unflinchingly optimistic. He is the God of hope, and He enables us to overflow with hope.

Trusting in Him is crucial to that equation. As Hebrews 10:23 says, "Let us hold unswervingly to the hope we profess, for he who promised is faithful." The key is holding on to hope, no matter what. We can do this because we believe God is faithful—not because we see results because after the results come, we do not need hope (see Romans 8:24). Paul praised the Thessalonian believers for their "endurance inspired by hope in our Lord Jesus Christ" (1 Thessalonians 1:3). Hope in God enables us to endure. It is what keeps us going in the waiting.

Hope is a powerful force, but once lost, it can be difficult to regain. In Proverbs it says, "Hope deferred makes the heart sick, but a longing fulfilled is a tree of life" (Proverbs 13:12). This is the natural reality, but God offers us a greater spiritual reality. Hope deferred *can* make the heart sick, but because of Christ, it doesn't have to. In Romans, Paul tells us, "Hope does not disappoint, because the love of God has been poured out within our hearts through the Holy Spirit" (Romans 5:5 NASB). In other words, even when we are in a season of waiting to see the fulfillment of our prayers, the love of Christ in our hearts can keep our hope strong. Even when we have experienced loss and disappointment, the love of Christ can heal those wounds and rebuild hope in our hearts.

This is so important. The alternative is to allow disappointment to steal our hope, which only leads to fear and unbelief. It is better to live with unanswered questions as far as why something did or did not happen than to give in to hopelessness and fear. That is the way to the sickness of the heart.

> *Do not be anxious about anything, but in every situation, by prayer and petition, with thanksgiving, present your requests to God. And the peace of God, which transcends all understanding, will guard your hearts and your minds in Christ Jesus.* (Philippians 4:6–7)

The answer to fear and worry is prayer, but we must not pray worry prayers that focus on the problems we see. We must pray hope-filled prayers, declaring God's Word over our children. When it comes to our children, it can be hard to not feel afraid because we love them deeply. To be effective intercessors for them, we must release them to God and trust in His goodness toward them. The Bible says, "It is God who works in [our children] to will and to act in order to fulfill his good purpose" (Philippians 2:13). We must reach the place where we can pray out of hope, not fear.

Romans 15:13 says the God of hope wants to fill us with joy and peace, which are the gateway to hope. These three go hand-in-hand. As we let go of trying to control our children and really trust in God's goodness, we will be able to step into His joy and peace. We will be able to laugh at the lies of the enemy and rest in God's faithfulness. And from that place, we will find our hearts overflowing with hope. As Paul says, "Be joyful in hope, patient in affliction, faithful in prayer" (Romans 12:12).

The Bible tells the story of Hannah, a woman who was barren, but who desperately wanted a child. She prayed earnestly for a son, and God gave her Samuel. After Samuel's birth, she said: "I prayed for this child, and the Lord has granted me what I asked of him. So now I give him to the Lord. For his whole life he will be given over to the Lord" (1 Samuel 1:27–28). Hannah surrendered her son to God and did as He told her to do. This allowed God full access to Samuel's life, and as a result, he became a great prophet. We must do the same with our children.

Anxiety and stress will only bring us down and weaken our faith. Instead, we must visualize ourselves going to the throne of God and giving our children to Him. We can carry the burden of our children in the spirit, but we are not to carry the worry and anxiety. Instead, we must choose to entrust our children to God and then agree in prayer with His will for their lives. God cares about our children, and He cares about us. Let us learn to lean on Him, as Peter says, and trust Him to bring the breakthrough we need.

Casting the whole of your care [all your anxieties, all your worries, all your concerns, once and for all] on Him, for He cares for you affectionately and cares about you watchfully.
(1 Peter 5:7 AMPC)

The Faith Mindset

The third mindset we need on this journey as parent intercessors is the mindset of faith. This may seem obvious, yet many of us struggle to maintain faith in prayer when we do not see the immediate manifestation of the answers. If hope is a general expectation that good things will happen in our lives when we follow Jesus, faith is belief in a specific promise from God of something good. This could be a promise from the Bible or a promise He has given us personally. So, hope is a big-picture optimism, and from that optimism springs faith for specific things.

Simply defined, *faith* **is believing God is who He says He is and He will do what He says He will do (see Hebrews 6:11). Faith is belief in specific promises from God.**

Abraham is called the father of faith because he gives us an incredible example of belief in God's word. God had promised Abraham and Sarah an heir, even though they were already past the age of childbearing. Abraham and Sarah believed God's promise and then kept believing for twenty-five years until their son Isaac was finally born.[61] Yes, both Abraham and Sarah had moments of unbelief, but their overall stance was one of faith in God's word, even when it was clearly impossible in the natural. Paul says that Abraham believed "against all hope" (Romans 4:18).

> *Without weakening in his faith, he faced the fact that his body was as good as dead—since he was about a hundred years old—and that Sarah's womb was also dead. Yet he did not waver through unbelief regarding the promise of God, but was strengthened in his faith and gave glory to God.* (Romans 4:19–20)

When God told Abraham, "I have made you a father of many nations," Abraham believed Him because he knew He was "the God who gives life to the dead and calls into being things that were not" (Romans 4:17). Abraham knew God *could* bring life into Sarah's barren and aged womb, and he believed that He *would* because He had promised it. He believed God had the ability, and He believed God would follow through on His promise. We must do the same, no matter how long we have been waiting to see the answer to our prayers. Delay is not denial. God is not saying no to prayers that align with His Word. He's not backing out of His promises either. He is always faithful.

Faith in Him is the fuel of our prayers. When a distraught father came to Jesus asking for healing for his son, Jesus corrected him for saying, "If you can do anything, take pity on us and help us" (Mark 9:22). His words were not filled with much faith, but with sorrow and despair. Jesus responded, "'If you can'? Everything is possible for one who believes" (Mark 9:23). The father, quickly recognizing his error, changed his words. "I do believe; help me overcome my unbelief!" (Mark 9:24).

We can learn a lot from this father. It can be very easy to slip into fear and anxiety when our kids are struggling, but fear is the enemy of faith. Paul says, "For no matter how many promises God has made, they are 'Yes' in Christ. And so through him the 'Amen' is spoken by us to the glory of God" (2 Corinthians 1:20). God's promises are always good. In Christ, we receive all He has promised us. When we pray in faith, we are saying *amen* to the promises God has made us. Another definition for faith is found in Hebrews 11:1.

> *Now faith is the assurance (title deed, confirmation) of things hoped for (divinely guaranteed), and the evidence of things not seen [the conviction of their reality—faith comprehends as fact what cannot be experienced by the physical senses].* (AMP)

Faith is certain, which means it isn't concerned about the circumstances, but instead looks at the promises of God. When we pray for our children, we must remember that feelings, behaviors, and circumstances may not accurately reflect what God is doing. This is why we must keep our focus on His promises, not on what we see around us. As Paul says, "So we fix our eyes not on what is seen, but on what is unseen, since what is seen is temporary, but what is unseen is eternal" (2 Corinthians 4:18). Sometimes things in the natural seem to get worse before they get better. This can happen for a variety of reasons, including stubbornness or disobedience in our children.

Our prayers are stirring things up in the spiritual realm, and the enemy doesn't like that. He doesn't like to give up easily, but our patient persistence will win out in the end. In Luke 4:33–36, Jesus rebuked an evil spirit that had taken possession of a man. Before the spirit left the man, it threw the man down to the ground. Then, it came out. The evil spirit knew it needed to leave, but it wanted to make a commotion first. This often happens when we exercise our authority in the spirit, but that "commotion" does not mean our authority isn't real or doesn't work. The enemy wants us to be intimidated and give up, but when we stand firm like Jesus, we will see deliverance and breakthrough.

When it comes it our kids, it can be easy to waiver because we see them at their worst moments at home and we are very emotionally attached to their situations. What we must remember if the seen realm seems to be getting worse, it means we are making progress in the unseen spirit realm. We must never judge the success of our prayers based on outward appearances. In Matthew 14:22–33, Peter stepped out of the boat in faith, but then he began to look at the wind and waves, and he slipped from faith into fear. As a result, he started to sink, until he called out to Jesus for help. Like Peter, we must keep our eyes on Jesus, the author and finisher of our children's destinies (see Hebrews 12:1–2; Philippians 1:6).

> **When we pray for our kids, we must choose to rise above our circumstances and come to God with hearts full of faith and hope in Him. We must place our faith in God's goodness and the promises He has made to us. When we abide in faith, without wavering (see James 1:6–8), we *will* see a breakthrough.**

We are the only ones who have authority in our homes. Let us, therefore, stand firm and unmovable, always abounding in the work of intercession, knowing our prayers are not in vain. Faith looks in the Spirit and believes before it sees in the natural.

I once heard Kenneth E. Hagin say faith is like a switch we can turn off or on, just like a light switch. When I walk into a dark room, I turn on the light switch, and I keep it on as long as I am in the room. This is the stance we need to take in faith. We will keep the faith switch *on* for as long as we need to in a particular "room" of prayer. When we find ourselves in the difficult position of waiting for the manifestation of what we have prayed for, we must simply choose to stand firm in faith and hope. We do this by choosing to believe our prayers are effective, no matter what we may see or feel in the natural.

> *Truly I tell you, if anyone says to this mountain, "Go, throw yourself into the sea," and does not doubt in their heart but believes that what they say will happen, it will be done for them. Therefore I tell you, whatever you ask for in prayer, believe that you have received it, and it will be yours.* (Jesus in Mark 11:23–24)

In this passage, the mountain is a symbol of any obstacle we face. In prayer for our children, faith looks like believing God's promises in our hearts and then declaring them with our mouths.

Notice, Jesus says such a person must believe "what they say will happen." Faith is not just an issue of the heart, but also of our words. In seasons when we are waiting for a breakthrough to come, it is very important to understand the laws of the Spirit. Life and death are in the power of our words. We must watch the words we speak to our children and about our children, especially when we feel frustrated. We must continually declare God's Word over our children—both in prayer and in day-to-day life—because life and death are in the power of the tongue (see Proverbs 18:1). If we are speaking negatively to or about our children, we will undermine our prayers on their behalf. Instead, our words must be unified toward a single goal—breakthrough and blessing for our children. We must not allow careless words to nullify our prayers. Instead, let's believe and speak according to what God says.

Likewise, in moments when we are struggling to believe, we must be careful not to express our doubt with words like, "Well, I guess God didn't hear me," or "Things are just getting worse." Words like these agree with the enemy and temporary circumstances, not with eternity. We want to position our words to agree with Heaven and what God says and believes about our children. This is not denial, but faith.

Faith doesn't deny the circumstances, but it does deny the circumstances the right to rule over God's promises.

A friend told me about the challenge of his son's teen years. It seemed like he was continually getting into trouble, and my friend was at his wit's end. He decided to start praying for his son every night before bed, but his prayers started to take the form of complaints. "Do You know what he did today, God?" he would say. Then he would list all the trouble his son was getting into. After some time, the Holy Spirit stopped him right in the middle of one of these "prayers" and said, "Do you think I don't know what you're telling me? I see everything that's going on and more than you know. Don't pray the problem; pray the answer." From that point on, my friend started praying about what he wanted to see in his son's life. Immediately, his attitude toward his son changed, and soon he began seeing a turnaround in his son. The words we speak show where we are putting our faith. Let's be careful to speak only what God speaks.

To see the power of faith-filled prayer, we simply need to look to the life of Daniel. Though Daniel was a captive in a heathen nation, he remained faithful to God in all things and served Him wholeheartedly. He is truly one of the great champions of the Bible. In chapter 10 of the Book of Daniel, we find Daniel in prayer and fasting. After twenty-one days, an angel appeared to Daniel and gave him a vision regarding the future of Israel. First, the angel explained why it took him twenty-one days to answer Daniel's prayers.

> *Do not be afraid, Daniel. Since the first day that you set your mind to gain understanding and to humble yourself before your God, your words were heard, and I have come in response to them. But the prince of the Persian kingdom resisted me twenty-one days. Then Michael, one of the chief princes, came to help me, because I was detained there with*

the king of Persia. Now I have come to explain to you what will happen to your people in the future, for the vision concerns a time yet to come. (Daniel 10:12–14)

We find several important truths here. First, God hears our prayers as soon as we pray. We don't have to put in a certain amount of prayer time before He takes notice. He hears us immediately. Second, when we experience delay, it is because of spiritual warfare. The resistance is not from God, but from the enemy. Third, if we stand in faith like Daniel, we will see the manifestation of our prayers. In the in-between, many lose heart and stop praying. Instead, like Daniel, we must patiently maintain our confession of faith before God.

God is not unjust; he will not forget your work and the love you have shown him as you have helped his people and continue to help them. We want each of you to show this same diligence to the very end, so that what you hope for may be fully realized. We do not want you to become lazy, but to imitate those who through faith and patience inherit what has been promised. (Hebrews 6:10–12)

God will not overlook our labor of love in prayer for our children. If we remain diligent and do not give up, what we hope for will be fully realized. The answer is coming, if we will just stand firm in faith, hope, and confidence in our victory.

Paul exhorts us, "Therefore, my dear brothers and sisters, stand firm. Let nothing move you. Always give yourselves fully to the work of the Lord, because you know that your labor in the Lord is not in vain" (1 Corinthians 15:58).

Intercession is hard work. It is a labor of love, but that labor is never in vain. Sometimes, the answers come quickly. At other times, we face hurdles in the spirit and need to persevere. No matter what, we must determine to never quit or faint. We must decide at the beginning we will keep praying, no matter how long it takes. We must learn to be stubborn in the Spirit and to "be strong in the Lord and in His mighty power" (Ephesians 6:10). The strength of God on the inside will enable us to stand and fight, no matter what may come.

Love never fails, and neither will we when we intercede for our children in faith, hope, and love.

Digging Deeper Workbook Chapter 16

The Victory Mindset

"We do not war *for* victory, as if it were up to our methods and works to obtain it. Rather we war *from* victory. We war *from* a position of intimacy with the Ultimate Victor, and are enforcing the victory He has already purchased." - Bill Johnson, *Hosting the Presence: Unveiling Heaven's Agenda*

Simply defined, the victory mindset is _____.

The Hope Mindset

We could say hope is the overarching belief that we can expect good things to happen in our lives. It is a relentless optimism based on the goodness of God, regardless of our circumstances.

Hebrews 10:23 says, "Let us hold unswervingly to the hope we profess, for he who promised is faithful." We must choose to entrust our children to God and then agree in prayer with His will for their lives.

God cares about our children, and He cares about us. Lean on Him and trust Him to bring the breakthrough we need.

Simply defined, the hope mindset is _____.

The Faith Mindset

> *Now faith is the assurance (title deed, confirmation) of things hoped for (divinely guaranteed), and the evidence of things not seen [the conviction of their reality—faith comprehends as fact what cannot be experienced by the physical senses].* (Hebrews 11:1 AMP)

Simply defined, *faith* is _____ that God is who He says He is and He will do what He says He will do (see Hebrews 6:11).

Faith is _____ in specific promises from God.

Believe God has the ability, and He will follow through on His promise.

Remember:
Delay is _____ denial.

God is not saying no to prayers that _____ with His _____.

He's _____ backing out of His promises.

He is _____ faithful.

Faith doesn't deny the _____, but it does deny the circumstances the right to _____ over God's promises.

*God is **not** unjust; he will **not** forget your work and the love you have shown him as you have helped his people and continue to help them. We want each of you to **show this same diligence** to the very end, so that what you hope for may be fully realized. We do not want you to become lazy, but to **imitate those who through faith and patience inherit what has been promised**.* (Hebrews 6:10–12 emphasis added)

Now Declare God's Word over Your children

We must watch the words we speak to our children and about our children, especially when we feel frustrated. We must continually declare God's Word over our children—both in prayer and in day-to-day life—because life and death are in the power of the tongue (see Proverbs 18:1).

Explain why this is so important:

_____

When we pray for our kids, we must choose to rise above our _____ and come to God with hearts full of _____ and _____ in Him. We must place our faith in God's goodness and the promises He has made to us. When we abide in faith, without wavering (see James 1:6–8), we _____ see a breakthrough.

Write Your Prayer for Your Child

Remember: Love never fails, and neither will we when we intercede for our children in faith, hope, and love.

Chapter 17
Practical Prayers for Our Children: Part 1

These prayers are rooted in the Bible and are aligned with the general will of God. Thus, we can know with certainty that when we pray for our children in this way, we are praying correctly and contending effectively for their hearts and destinies in prayer.

Obviously, to pray in agreement with God's will, we first need to know His will. Hosea 4:6 says people can be destroyed by a lack of knowledge. A lack of understanding regarding God's Word and His will can open the door for destruction in our families. However, if we know what God's will is, then we are equipped to fight for it through intercession. Knowledge of the Bible builds faith and confidence in our hearts thus stabilizing us in hope, no matter what is happening around us (see Romans 10:17).

In Romans 1:16, Paul says, "For I am not ashamed of the gospel, because it is the power of God that brings salvation to everyone who believes." The Greek word used for salvation is *soteria*, which means "salvation, healing, deliverance, safety and soundness, welfare, prosperity, and preservation."[62] It is salvation in a holistic sense. It includes every area of our lives, not just our eternal destination.

God longs for every person to come into a relationship with Him and to be saved from their sins, but He doesn't stop there. He also longs to bring them into health and abundance in every area. Knowing this empowers us to declare the full gospel and will of God over our children.

God's Will for Eternal Salvation

God loves the whole world, and He sent Jesus to redeem the whole world to Him. Jesus has already provided eternal life and all the benefits of salvation for every person, yet many have rejected Him or have never heard the good news. This is our biggest priority as parents. We are to pray our children would encounter the love of God and receive His gift of salvation. To the jailer at Philippi, Paul said, "Believe in the Lord Jesus, and you will be saved—you and your household" (Acts 16:31). We can claim this promise for ourselves and that all our children will be saved and walk with God because that is His will for their lives (see 1 Timothy 2:4; 2 Peter 3:9).

Being raised in a Christian home and going to church regularly does not guarantee our children are saved. An increasing percentage of young people are leaving the Church after they move out of their parent's homes. It is more important than ever to pray our children would encounter God's love in a life-changing way and cultivate their relationship with Him. We can teach them the right things and be great examples, but ultimately, each of our kids needs to encounter God for themselves. They need their own relationship with Him, based on their own conviction and choices.

In Psalm 2:8, God promises, "Ask me, and I will make the nations your inheritance, the ends of the earth your possession." God was not talking about physically possessing people and places. Instead, He was promising spiritual territory. He was promising that when we pray for salvation, He will bring in the harvest. When praying for our kids' salvation, we can begin with declaring scriptures over them. We also have the authority to call them to come and be saved in the name of Jesus (see John 14:14; Mark 16:17). Our prayers also release the ministry of the Holy Spirit, who works to convict and convince them of their need for Jesus (see John 16:7–11 AMP).

We can also pray God would send people into our kids' lives who can connect with them and be a witness to them of the love of God (see Matthew 9:38). God will do it. He knows the perfect people to relate to our children. The Bible says he who wins souls is wise (see Proverbs 11:30). God is the ultimate winner of souls, and He has great wisdom in how and who can reach our children.

In His parable about the different types of soil, Jesus showed us that people's hearts are like soil. They don't all respond in the same way to the seed of God's Word. Some receive it quickly. Others need more time. The soil of the hearts of our children is in large part determined by their life experiences. Trauma, disappointment, betrayal, and hardship can cause rocks or thorns in their hearts, which may make it harder for them to receive the seed of God's Word. When we pray for them, our prayers act like a plow tilling the soil of their hearts, so when the seed of the Word of God is sown, it will be received into their hearts and bring forth fruit (see Mark 4:14–20).

Wisdom and Revelation

In Paul's letter to the church at Ephesus, we find a prayer for his spiritual children.

> *I have not stopped giving thanks for you, remembering you in my prayers. I keep asking that the God of our Lord Jesus Christ, the glorious Father, may give you the Spirit of wisdom and revelation, so that you may know him better. I pray that the eyes of your heart may be enlightened in order that you may know the hope to which he has called you, the riches of his glorious inheritance in his holy people, and his*

incomparably great power for us who believe. That power is the same as the mighty strength he exerted when he raised Christ from the dead and seated him at his right hand in the heavenly realms. (Ephesians 1:16–20)

Like Paul, we can pray for wisdom and revelation for our children. The word for wisdom here, *sophia*, refers to insight into the true nature of things. *Revelation* specifically refers to a revealing of something that was once hidden. I like to think of it as opening a curtain so we can see what is behind it. We all need deepening and ongoing revelation of God as we grow in our relationship with Him.

We all should regularly experience "ah-ha" moments in which what once seemed hard to understand is now clear. This happens when the Holy Spirit opens our spiritual eyes regarding a particular truth. Revelation also takes what we might know in our heads and makes it a living truth in our hearts. It's the heart knowledge that enables us to live according to that truth because that sort of revelation changes us.

We see this in the story of the disciples who encountered Jesus on the road to Emmaus. While Jesus talked with them, He opened their understanding so they would comprehend with their hearts the truth of the scriptures they had read many times before (see Luke 24:45). In the same way, we should pray that the eyes of our children's hearts would be opened to the truth of the Word of God.

God wants to reveal His truth to them—including the truth of His nature and His love for them. In Ephesians 1, Paul says the whole purpose of the spirit of wisdom and revelation is to help us know God better. This is what He wants for our children. A revelation of who God is and His love for them will change everything. It is not surprising that Paul also prayed specifically for a revelation of God's love in the hearts of his spiritual children.

I pray that you, being rooted and established in love, may have power, together with all the Lord's holy people, to grasp how wide and long and high and deep is the love of Christ, and to know this love that surpasses knowledge—that you may be filled to the measure of all the fullness of God. (Ephesians 3:17–19)

A revelation of God's love is the greatest revelation of all because it is a revelation of God Himself. The Bible tells us love is not just an attribute of God; it is His identity. As the apostle John says, "And so we know and rely on the love God has for us. God is love. Whoever lives in love lives in God, and God in them" (1 John 4:16). A revelation of God's love enables us to live in communion with Him. The revelation comes first. Without this revelation, our children will have a hard time knowing God, and they will also have a hard time seeing themselves the way He sees them.

The Bible tells us God's love drives out the fear and insecurity in our lives. "There is no fear in love. But perfect love drives out fear because fear has to do with punishment. The one who fears is not made perfect in love" (1 John 4:18). Fear is an indicator that our revelation of God's love is lacking. Children who need a revelation of God's love often exhibit not only fear, but also insecurity, addiction, eating disorders, and self-harm. All these are manifestations of fear, which lead to self-hatred. Such children may also feel condemned all the time like they never measure up, and they may struggle to form lasting friendships. Often, they have an exaggerated sense of rejection from others.[63]

Our children desperately need to know they are loved and chosen. Lack of knowledge of God's love causes people to perish spiritually, emotionally, and even physically (see Hosea 4:6). Social media has only increased the opportunities for bullying and peer pressure in our kids' lives. The answer is a revelation of their belonging with God.

Only this will truly set them free from fear, insecurity, and depression. Jesus promises, "Then you will know the truth, and the truth will set you free" (John 8:32). As they begin to understand His nature and His heart toward them, they will learn how to walk in confidence and peace.

We can pray our children would receive a revelation of the *agape* (unconditional) love of God for them. What God is like, as the embodiment of love, is defined in 1 Corinthians 13:4–8. His love is greater than the love of any human. His love is so great that He gave His own life for ours (see Romans 5:8). The value of anything is determined by what someone is willing to pay for it. Jesus forever determined our value when He paid His own life to redeem ours.

We can also pray our children would hear God speak His love to their hearts. He is calling to them, declaring, "I have chosen you and have not rejected you" (Isaiah 41:9), "I have loved you with an everlasting love; I have drawn you with unfailing kindness" (Jeremiah 31:3), and "I will not forget you!" (Isaiah 49:15). Hearing these words from their Father in Heaven is a revelation that will forever change our children. God is always speaking His love. We need to pray that the eyes and ears of our children would be open to perceiving it.

This was a continual prayer I prayed for Danielle during the ten years when she was struggling. Although I did not know why the Holy Spirit kept prompting me to pray for a revelation of His love in her life. I believe the major encounter she experienced when she was instantly set free was a result of praying this prayer over her. It took ten years for those fiery darts to stop, but thankfully now we see the manifested result.

Visions, Dreams, and Encounters

Visions, dreams, and encounters are all types of revelation. If the wisdom and revelation Paul talks about in Ephesians 1 are like a still, small voice on the inside, visions, dreams, and encounters can be as dramatic as Saul's conversion on the road to Damascus (see Acts 9:1–15). Many books have been written on visions, dreams, and encounters, so I will not spend a lot of time defining these experiences here. What matters is that we find a clear biblical precedent for these in the lives of believers and even unbelievers. The Old Testament contains many stories of prophets and kings who had these experiences. Apparently, dreaming was so common for David that he wrote, "I will praise the LORD, who counsels me; even at night, my heart instructs me" (Psalm 16:7).

> *For God does speak—now one way, now another—though no one perceives it. In a dream, in a vision of the night, when deep sleep falls on people as they slumber in their beds, he may speak in their ears and terrify them with warnings, to turn them from wrongdoing and keep them from pride.* (Job 33:14–17)

Further, the apostles Paul, Peter, John, and various others in the New Testament had visions, dreams, and encounters. God still speaks in these ways today under the new covenant. As with Saul, who later became Paul, sometimes He uses them to shock our children into seeing the truth and turning toward Him. Saul was going his own way, completely convinced of what he was doing, until he encountered Jesus. Then his entire life changed. I have at times, called for an apprehension! "Lord, apprehend my children like You did with Saul on the road to Damascus."

Sometimes, God uses dreams to bring wisdom and conviction into our children's hearts when they are sleeping and, therefore, are more open to His influence. I know a parent whose child learned how to speak in tongues in a dream. God can do anything. He holds our children's hearts in His hands (see Proverbs 21:1), and He can direct them toward Him. We simply need to open that door for influence in prayer.

A Heart after God

Along with praying for revelation and encounters for our children, we should also pray they would develop a heart after God. We can pray that, like the prophet Samuel, they would learn early in life to obey the voice of their heavenly Father and thereby receive the desires of their hearts (see 1 Samuel 15:22). We can declare over them, "Surely then you will find delight in the Almighty and will lift up your face to God" (Job 22:26).

To prepare them to properly respond to difficult and hard times, we can pray that their eyes and hearts would always be fixed on God.

Under King Jehoshaphat, Judah was attacked by several enemy armies. Instead of relying on their own power and wisdom, Jehoshaphat acknowledged their need for God's intervention, and he prayed, "We have no power to face this vast army that is attacking us. We do not know what to do, but our eyes are on you" (2 Chronicles 20:12). He kept his eyes on God, even in the midst of trial, and as a result, he received God's help. In response to the king's prayer, God reassured the people, saying, "Do not be afraid; do not be discouraged. Go out to face them tomorrow, and the LORD will be with you" (2 Chronicles 20:17). The next day, Jehoshaphat and the army of Judah went out to face the enemy, and they sang worship songs to the Lord as they went. When they arrived on the battlefield, they found the enemy armies had destroyed one another, and not a single soldier had survived. God fought and won the battle for them because they kept their eyes on Him.

Along these same lines, Paul implored his spiritual children, "Live a life worthy of the calling you have received" (Ephesians 4:1). Though we are saved by faith, and not by works, God's desire for us is that we would grow up in Him and do good works for the Kingdom. He wants our lives to testify of His goodness and love. He calls us to "live a life worthy of the Lord and please him in every way: bearing fruit in every good work, growing in the knowledge of God" (Colossians 1:10).

> *We constantly pray for you, that our God may make you worthy of his calling, and that by his power he may bring to fruition your every desire for goodness and your every deed prompted by faith.* (2 Thessalonians 1:11)

Let us pray and declare that our children will have hearts after God and seek to obey Him in all they do, like King David, will live as people after God's heart (see Jeremiah 24:7; 1 Kings 9:4; Acts 13:22).

Christ-like Character

God's desire for our kids is not just that they would have hearts after Him, but also that they would continually grow in godly character (see Galatians 4:19). The two go together. The Bible says that as we behold God, we become like Him (see 2 Corinthians 3:18). So, if our children are pursuing God, they will also be growing in maturity. Still, it is important to pray for specific areas of maturity that are lacking or under-developed in our kids.

Paul lists the fruit of the Spirit in Galatians 5:22–23, "love, joy, peace, forbearance, kindness, goodness, faithfulness, gentleness and self-control." These are just as important in our kids' lives as the gifts of the Spirit. Either one without the other distorts our representation of God.

In 1 Corinthians 13, Paul says that love is the most important thing of all. It is the essence of who God is and the gospel message. If we perform miracles, operate in our spiritual gifts, or do good works without God-inspired love, those works are empty. We must pray our children would learn to love first, and that genuine love would be the foundation for everything they do for God.

Along with that, ask God to put His sense of justice in our children's hearts, that they would have compassion for the poor and oppressed, stand up for what is right, and defend the weak (see Isaiah 1:17). Compassionate love is a hallmark of the gospel, and it should be evident in the lives of all believers.

Supernatural Power and Miracles

Another important aspect of the Christian life is supernatural power. When Jesus ascended into Heaven, He told the disciples, "But you will receive power when the Holy Spirit comes on you, and you will be my witnesses" (Acts 1:8). Power was the important precursor to ministry then, and it still is today. Paul even went so far as to say, "The kingdom of God is not a matter of talk but of power" (1 Corinthians 4:1). When describing his ministry, Paul said he did what he did "in truthful speech and in the power of God" (2 Corinthians 6:7).

We cannot have the gospel without power, and neither can our kids. Jesus rebuked the Pharisees for their ignorance of God's power, saying, "You are in error because you do not know the Scriptures or the power of God" (Matthew 22:29). He directly connected their theological error to their lack of understanding, not only of the Scriptures but also of God's power.

We must pray that our children would see God's power at work in their lives so their "faith might not rest on human wisdom, but on God's power" (1 Corinthians 2:5). We must also pray they would learn to walk in His power. When Paul prayed for his spiritual children, he included a revelation of God's power in his requests.

I pray that the eyes of your heart may be enlightened in order that you may know...his incomparably great power for us who believe. That power is the same as the mighty strength he exerted when he raised Christ from the dead and seated him at his right hand in the heavenly realms. (Ephesians 1:18–20)

The power of God at work in our lives is the same power that raised Jesus from the dead. He has given us spiritual gifts, which are all demonstrations of His power. One of the spiritual gifts listed in 1 Corinthians 12 is even called "miraculous powers" (1 Corinthians 12:10). Not only that, but He has given us spiritual weapons to fight against the enemy. These spiritual weapons "have divine power to demolish strongholds" (2 Corinthians 10:4).

Our children have a great call to walk in miracles and supernatural power. The world is hungry for a generation that is truly walking in the power of God. To see them released into their destiny in this area, we must pray and declare specifically for an increase in supernatural power in their lives. Our children are destined to perform signs and wonders for the glory of God!

Physical Healing

Another important area of prayer for our kids is for their physical health. The Bible makes it clear God's blessing on our lives includes physical health and well-being. One of the signs of the Israelites' covenant with God was they did not suffer from the same sicknesses the Egyptians and other nations did (see Exodus 15:26). Their blessing was contingent on their obedience, and when they did not obey, they came under a curse (see Deuteronomy 28). However, Jesus removed the curse of sickness when He died on the cross (see Galatians 3:13; 1 Peter 2:24). Now, under the new covenant, the blessing of good health is still available to us. Hebrews 13:8 declares that Jesus is the same yesterday, today, and forever. He will never stop being our healer.

While He was on earth, healing of physical illness was one of the hallmarks of Jesus' ministry (see Matthew 9:35; Acts 10:38). The Bible even tells us several stories of parents bringing their sick children to Jesus and interceding for their healing. Jairus, a Jewish religious leader, came to Jesus and begged Him to come to his house and heal His deathly ill daughter. He said, "My little daughter is dying. Please come and put your hands on her so that she will be healed and live" (Mark 5:23). On the way, they learned the girl had already died. At this news, Jesus turned to Jairus and said, "Don't be afraid; just believe" (Mark 5:36). Then, Jesus raised her back to life. He is willing and eager to do the same for our children today. When our children face sickness or injury, His words to Jairus should ring in our ears—Don't be afraid; just believe! When James declared, "The prayer of a righteous person is powerful and effective" (James 5:16), he said it in the context of healing. It is God's will for our children to be physically healthy. Let us partner with Him by praying for their total health in Jesus' name.

Protection and Long Life

Not only does God want our children to be healthy, but He also wants them to be safe and to live long lives. Psalm 91 talks about how God protects His children, and I often pray it over my children. I pray He would keep them safe, protect them from harm, and send His angels to watch over them (see Psalm 91:16; Hebrews 1:14). I especially prayed this psalm over my children when they first began to drive. Now even as experience drivers, I pray this over them when they embark on a long trip in the car. Along these lines, Jesus prayed for His followers, "Holy Father, protect them by the power of your name, the name you gave me, so that they may be one as we are one" (John 17:11). Paul promised the early believers, "The Lord is faithful, and he will strengthen you and protect you from the evil one" (2 Thessalonians 3:3). This prayer and promises still apply today, and we can pray them over our children.

I also pray for protection over my children related to their relationships. Our children can easily be led down a bad road by friends who are a bad influence. Paul warns us, "Do not be yoked together with unbelievers. For what do righteousness and wickedness have in common? Or what fellowship can light have with darkness?" (2 Corinthians 6:14). For this reason, it is important to pray for our kids' friendships. Our children can often be very vulnerable in the area of friends. They desperately want to be liked and accepted, and this need for acceptance with their peers can be an open door to negative behaviors and beliefs.

Occasionally, my children did form friendships I had reservations about. It was not because I didn't like these friends, but because I didn't like the type of influence he or she had on my child or what the combination of that child and mine produced. When this happened, I always took my concerns to God. I would pray, "Lord, if this friend is not planted by You, I ask that this friendship would be uprooted" (see Matthew 15:13). Proverbs 12:26 says, "The righteous choose their friends carefully, but the way of the wicked leads them astray." As parents, we must pray relational protection over our children and declare they will choose their friends wisely.

When our family moved and when our kids left for college or moved to another state, I especially prayed God would bring the right relationships into their lives at the right time. The Bible says, "As iron sharpens iron, so one person sharpens another" (Proverbs 27:17). The right friendships can bring out the best in our children, and the wrong friendships can bring them down the wrong path. I also pray for the friends of my children, as these friends do have an influence on my kids' lives, and I want that influence to be good.

Over the years, many of my kids' friends have looked to me as a godmother, and I believe it is because I have invested in them spiritually through prayer. As a result, I gained even more influence into their lives and became a safe place for them.

God wants our kids to be safe physically and to live long and fulfilling lives. He also wants them to have good relationships that will be a blessing and spur them on in their walk with Him.

Digging Deeper Workbook Chapter 17

Practical Prayers for Our Children
Part One

Based on what you learned in this chapter, write a prayer for each of these areas. Leave a blank where you can insert the name of the child (natural or spiritual) you are praying for.

Salvation

> "Believe in the Lord Jesus, and you will be saved—you and your household." (Acts 16:31)

Your prayers release the ministry of the Holy Spirit, who works to convict and convince your child of their need for Jesus (see John 16:7–11 AMP). Also, pray God would send people into your kid's life who can connect with them and be a witness to them of the love of God (see Matthew 9:38).

Wisdom and Revelation

> *I have not stopped giving thanks for you, remembering you in my prayers. I keep asking that the God of our Lord*

Jesus Christ, the glorious Father, may give you the Spirit of wisdom and revelation, so that you may know him better. I pray that the eyes of your heart may be enlightened in order that you may know the hope to which he has called you, the riches of his glorious inheritance in his holy people, and his incomparably great power for us who believe. That power is the same as the mighty strength he exerted when he raised Christ from the dead and seated him at his right hand in the heavenly realms. (Ephesians 1:16–20)

I pray that you, being rooted and established in love, may have power, together with all the Lord's holy people, to grasp how wide and long and high and deep is the love of Christ, and to know this love that surpasses knowledge—that you may be filled to the measure of all the fullness of God. (Ephesians 3:17–19)

Pray that the eyes of your child's heart would be opened to the truth of the Word of God. Your child also needs a revelation of God's love. Pray that your child would receive a revelation of the *agape* (unconditional) love of God for them.

Visions, Dreams, and Encounters

For God does speak—now one way, now another—though no one perceives it. In a dream, in a vision of the night, when deep sleep falls on people as they slumber in their beds, he may speak in their ears and terrify them with warnings, to turn them from wrongdoing and keep them from pride. (Job 33:14–17)

Sometimes God uses dreams to bring wisdom and conviction into our child's heart when they are sleeping and, therefore, are more open to His influence.

A Heart after God

Along with praying for revelation and encounters for your child, also pray they would develop a heart after God. We can pray, that like the prophet Samuel, they would learn early in life to obey the voice of their heavenly Father and thereby receive the desires of their hearts

Declare over them, "Surely then you will find delight in the Almighty and will lift up your face to God" (Job 22:26).

Pray for your child like Paul did: "We constantly pray for you, that our God may make you worthy of his calling, and that by his power he may bring to fruition your every desire for goodness and your every deed prompted by faith" (2 Thessalonians 1:11).

Pray and declare your child will have a heart after God and seek to obey Him in all they do and live as a person after God's heart (see 1 Kings 9:4; Acts 13:22).

Godly Character

God's desire for our kids is not just that they would have hearts after Him, but also that they would continually grow in godly character.

Pray for specific areas of maturity that are lacking or under-developed in your child (Galatians 5:22–23: "love, joy, peace, forbearance, kindness, goodness, faithfulness, gentleness and self-control").

Pray your child would learn to love first and that genuine love would be the foundation for everything they do for God. Also, ask God to put His sense of justice in your child's heart, that they would have compassion for the poor and oppressed, stand up for what is right, and defend the weak (see Isaiah 1:17).

Supernatural Power

Pray your child would see God's power at work in their lives so their "faith might not rest on human wisdom, but on God's power" (1 Corinthians 2:5).

Pray they would learn to walk in His power.

> *I pray that the eyes of your heart may be enlightened in order that you may know…his incomparably great power for us who believe. That power is the same as the mighty strength he exerted when he raised Christ from the dead and seated him at his right hand in the heavenly realms.* (Ephesians 1:18–20)

Your child has a great call to walk in miracles and supernatural power. The world is hungry for a generation that is truly walking in the power of God. To see them released into their destiny in this area. Pray and declare specifically for an increase in supernatural power in their lives.

Health

It is God's will for your child to be physically healthy. Partner with Him by praying for their total health in Jesus' name. Remember, Jesus turned to Jairus and said, "Don't be afraid; just believe" (Mark 5:36).

Protection and Long Life

Psalm 91 talks about how God protects His children. Pray for God to keep your child safe, protect your child from harm, and send His angels to watch over them (see Psalm 91:16; Hebrews 1:14).

Pray for relational protection over your child and declare they will choose their friends wisely. "Lord, if this friend is not planted by You, I ask that this friendship would be uprooted" (see Matthew 15:13). Proverbs 12:26 says, "The righteous choose their friends carefully, but the way of the wicked leads them astray." The right friendships can bring out the best in your child, and the wrong friendships can bring them down the wrong path.

God wants your child to be safe physically and to live a long and fulfilling life. He also wants them to have good relationships that will be a blessing and spur them on in their walk with Him.

Chapter 18
Practical Prayers for Our Children: Part 2

Provision

God wants to provide for our children in the natural. This applies to our adult children who are spreading their wings outside of our homes. Paul promised us, "And my God will meet all your needs according to the riches of his glory in Christ Jesus" (Philippians 4:19). We can cling to this promise and ask God for provision for our families, as well as wisdom to make great financial decisions and strategies for financial increase. God has all the wisdom we need, and He wants to help us, and our children to thrive and prosper in all areas, including our finances.

Open Doors and Favor

Another way we can pray for provision for our children is to pray for open doors and favor—for the right college or job or whatever they need to position themselves to reach their destinies. David testifies about the favor of the Lord, "Surely, Lord, you bless the righteous; you surround them with your favor as with a shield" (Psalm 5:12). God wants to surround our children with the shield of His favor, which will protect them from attacks against their calling. Favor causes us to have unreasonable influence or access. It opens doors that, naturally speaking, we might not deserve to have opened. It can elevate us to positions of influence more rapidly than usual. Favor looks like Daniel and Joseph miraculously being promoted to positions of authority within godless and evil kingdoms—without compromising their convictions or faith. This is what we want for our kids as they pursue education, careers, athletics, and so forth.

We see this principle at work in Paul's life. Paul was called to be an apostle of the gospel, and he traveled to places where he had no influence and attempted to preach the gospel. Because he had no natural reason to have favor with people, he asked other believers to pray that God would open doors of favor before him: "And pray for us, too, that God may open a door for our message, so that we may proclaim the mystery of Christ" (Colossians 4:3).

In other places, Paul testified God gave him favor in his missionary work. To the Corinthians, he wrote that "a great door for effective work" had been opened for him in Ephesus (1 Corinthians 16:9). He also testified that when he went to Troas he "found that the Lord had opened a door" for him (2 Corinthians 2:12). Whatever calling God has given our children, we can assist them by praying God would open doors of favor so they can fulfill their calling.

In the Book of Revelation, Jesus says to the believers at the church of Philadelphia: "I have placed before you an open door that no one can shut" (Revelation 3:8). The full name of this book is The Revelation of Jesus; in other words, its purpose is to show us what the risen Jesus is like. Here we find that Jesus is the one who makes a way where there is no way and opens doors that can't be shut. As Isaiah prophesied about Jesus, "I will place on his shoulder the key to the house of David; what he opens no one can shut, and what he shuts no one can open" (Isaiah 22:22). The church in Philadelphia was faithful to the gospel, even under horrible persecution, and Jesus was promising to provide an open door for them. Though the passage doesn't specify what that open door was, it seems to indicate that it was related to deliverance from those who were persecuting them.

When our children face tough times, we can also pray that God would open a door of deliverance for them. He is able to open doors of deliverance, favor, and promotion for our children that no one can close.

A Strong, Creative Mind

Another important prayer for our children is that they would have strong, creative minds. In Exodus 35, we find the story of Bezalel, who is the first person the Bible specifically says was filled with the Spirit of God. Moses said, "He [God] has filled him [Bezalel] with the Spirit of God, with wisdom, with understanding, with knowledge and with all kinds of skills" (Exodus 30:31). God filled Bezalel with His Spirit to enhance his mind so he could oversee the workmanship involved in making the tabernacle.

God is the Creator, and He made us in His image to be creative people. He wants our minds to be strong and useful. Today, the advent of smartphones and the ever-present technology in our lives can pose a threat to our children's intellects. While we can't make our children completely avoid technology, we can pray God would strengthen and quicken their minds so they would have ease in learning, possess a good memory, and be creative and imaginative thinkers.

Part of the Holy Spirit's role in our lives is to teach and remind us (see John 14:26). In other words, He strengthens our minds. When we are filled with the Holy Spirit, one of the outcomes will be the soundness of mind (see 2 Timothy 1:7). Just as God has made peace, joy, hope, and so many other things available to believers, He has also made mental health and strength available. If our children struggle with anxiety, depression, or any other mental illness, we can claim these promises and declare that their minds are made whole and healthy by the blood of Jesus. The enemy wants to lie to them and cause their minds to turn against them, but the truth is the Spirit of God has provided healing for their minds.

Jesus said, "I have come that they may have life, and that they may have it more abundantly" (John 10:10). The life He talks about here is the life of God. The Greek word used here, *zoë*, means "the absolute fulness of life, both essential and ethical, which belongs to God." This divine life is much more than eternal salvation. It involves giving the fullness of life to every area of our lives, including quickening our minds. Paul says, "If the Spirit of Him who raised Jesus from the dead dwells in you, He who raised Christ from the dead will also give life to your mortal bodies through His Spirit who dwells in you" (Romans 8:11).

The same power that raised Jesus from the dead gives *zoë* life to our bodies, including our minds. Whether our children are in school or in the workforce, we can pray God would strengthen their minds, give them creative ideas, help them to focus, and have an excellent memory.

Courage, Strength, and Peace

Along these same lines, we should pray for courage, strength, and peace. God cares for our children and does not want them to struggle with fear, worry, and anxiety (see Matthew 6:25–33). The Spirit of God does not give them fear. Instead, His love gives them peace and courage for life (see 2 Timothy 1:7; 1 Peter 5:7). Pray they will "be strong in the Lord and in his mighty power" (Ephesians 6:10). Declare over them the promise of Hebrews 13:6, "The Lord is my helper; I will not be afraid. What can mere mortals do to me." If they really believe this, it will change everything for them. Our children need inner strength from the Spirit to face life with courage and peace.

We can help them find it by praying and declaring it over them. We can pray God would give them the strength to do what they need to do each day (see Philippians 4:13). We can pray they know God cares for them and learn to cast their cares on Him (see 1 Peter 5:7). He alone can give them the comfort they need. Paul counsels us, "Do not be anxious about anything, but in every situation, by prayer and petition, with thanksgiving, present your requests to God" (Philippians 4:6). We can pray our children would follow this advice and learn to lean into God when they feel anxious and afraid.

We can pray they would be brave as they face the challenges before them (see Joshua 1:9). We can declare to their spirits the words Moses said to Joshua when he handed him the leadership of Israel: "Be strong and courageous. Do not be afraid or terrified because of them, for the LORD your God goes with you; he will never leave you nor forsake you" (Deuteronomy 31:6). We can ask God to help their hearts to be calm and peaceful as they go through their days and in their sleep at night.

Paul prayed for his spiritual children in Colossae that they would be strengthened with God's might so they could "have great endurance and patience" (Colossians. 1:11). He also wrote to the Ephesians, "I pray that out of his glorious riches he may strengthen you with power through his Spirit in your inner being, so that Christ may dwell in your hearts through faith" (Ephesians 3:16–17).

God's will for His children is we would all learn to live in the peace He has already provided for us, no matter what our circumstances. As parents, we can pray our children would receive a revelation of God's peace and learn how to step into His peace in all circumstances.

Obedience to the Will of God

Another important prayer is for obedient hearts. The older our kids get, the more we need to pray the Lord will lead them as they begin to make an increasing number of decisions independently. The

Bible counsels us to "trust in the LORD with all your heart and lean not on your own understanding; in all your ways submit to him, and he will make your paths straight" (Proverbs 3:5–6). We must pray our children would learn to discern the will of God and then choose to obey His will. We can echo the prayer Paul made for the Colossians.

> *We continually ask God to fill you with the knowledge of his will through all the wisdom and understanding that the Spirit gives, so that you may live a life worthy of the Lord and please him in every way: bearing fruit in every good work, growing in the knowledge of God.* (Colossians 1:9–10)

We see the first step to walking in God's will is having wisdom and understanding to know what His will is. This knowledge then enables us to live lives that are pleasing to God and bear spiritual fruit.

Later in the same letter, Paul told the believers at Colossae that another believer, Epaphras, continually interceded for them that they would obey God's will, "He is always wrestling in prayer for you, that you may stand firm in all the will of God, mature and fully assured" (Colossians 4:12). The Greek word for laboring is *panos*, which means "to fight, to struggle, often an athletic contest, labors, toil, distress, suffering pain." This is the prayer of intercession. Epaphras was contending and laboring in prayer on behalf of others. Here, he was specifically interceding that they would not just know God's will, but that they would also walk in obedience to it.

This is a prayer all parents should pray. If our children are believers, He has put within them the grace, or divine power, to live according to His will. As Peter says, "His divine power has given us everything we need for a godly life through our knowledge of him who called us by his own glory and goodness" (2 Peter 1:3).

Our kids have what it takes to live in alignment with the will of God. They have the ability to succeed in this, but they also have the freedom to disobey. Thus, our prayer should be that they would not only discern God's will, but also choose to follow it.

Manifestation of Their Destiny

As parents, we should also pray our children would walk into their destiny. Every child is born with a unique destiny and purpose on this earth. Part of our job as parents is to pray that destiny into being. Our children don't start out walking in their destiny from birth. Instead, they embark on a journey designed to bring them to maturity so they can fulfill their divine calling. As we pray for our children, we should pray that what God has placed on the inside of them would manifest on the outside. We can call forth their destiny and the good that is already inside them in Jesus' name (see Ecclesiastes 3:11).

The Bible tells us God placed our gifts within us in the womb, and He knew our destiny before we were born. When God called Jeremiah as His prophet, He told him, "Before I formed you in the womb I knew you, before you were born I set you apart; I appointed you as a prophet to the nations" (Jeremiah 1:5). The same is true for all people. Before our children were even conceived, God knew them and set them apart for a particular calling and destiny. He also placed within them unique gifting, personality, and love language because each of these plays a part in a person's destiny.

Similarly, David says, "Your eyes saw my unformed body; all the days ordained for me were written in your book before one of them came to be" (Psalm 139:16). I like to put my children's names in Psalm 139 and declare it out loud as a prophetic decree over their lives. God has lovingly designed our children's calling in this life. We should pray they would yield to their gifting from the womb and be true to their destiny according to what is written in Heaven.

We can pray that God the Father, the Master Potter, would mold our children according to His will (see Jeremiah 18:1–6).

Jesus taught us to pray, "Our Father in heaven, hallowed be your name, your kingdom come, your will be done, on earth as it is in heaven" (Matthew 6:9–10). We can apply this to our children by praying that what God has ordained for them in Heaven would manifest on earth.

I also like to declare Jeremiah 29:11 over them. "'For I know the plans I have for you,' declares the Lord, 'plans to prosper you and not to harm you, plans to give you hope and a future.'" God has good plans for our children's lives. Let's agree with Him that those plans will happen, and no attack of the enemy will keep our kids from walking in their destiny.

A Blessed Future

Lastly, along with praying for our children's destiny, we can also pray for a blessed future. This encompasses more than their calling in life and includes all their life decisions and situations. It may take them years to reach the place where they are fully walking in their calling. However, God wants them to experience His blessing at every step along the way.

Blessing our children's future obviously encompasses many of the previous prayer points in this chapter, but it is also a catch-all sort of prayer that covers every aspect of their future, including the things we might not think of. Most things regarding the future are a mystery, so praying in tongues can be very useful when we pray for our children's future. I call it "praying it forward"—when we pray ahead of things on their behalf.

The Old Testament prophet Isaiah prophesied about John the Baptist and how he would prepare the way for Jesus in the Spirit.

> *In the wilderness prepare the way for the Lord; make straight in the desert a highway for our God. Every valley shall be raised up, every mountain and hill made low; the*

rough ground shall become level, the rugged places a plain. And the glory of the LORD *will be revealed.* (Isaiah 40:3–5)

Like John the Baptist, we can also prepare a way for our children in the Spirit through our prayers. John prepared people's hearts to hear the truth, and through our intercession, we can spiritually prepare our children's hearts to receive the truth of the Word of God (see Mark 4:1–20). We can declare straight paths, valleys raised up, mountains made low, and rough ground made smooth for them in the name of Jesus. We can be like spiritual trailblazers who go ahead and mark the trail and remove obstacles. If the way has not been prepared, then the road ahead will be rough and hard, but if we prepare the way, we create an avenue for God's truth and blessing to flow in their lives. Life is not always easy. Sometimes it can be very hard.

Powerful Parenting Insights

➢ When children have praying parents, potential traps and difficulties can be thwarted or absorbed by the blanket of prayer.
➢ This prayer covering smooths out the road by removing and reducing obstacles to success, and it helps to make the way plain.

It takes a lot of work to build a highway in the natural, and it also takes work in the spirit. In intercession, we become laborers with God (see 2 Corinthians 6:1) to prepare the way for our children's success in life.

Consider this. If I am driving along a road that is crooked and windy and goes through many valleys and mountains, it will take more effort on my part to reach my destination. I will need to concentrate closely on the road, and I'll need to brake often when descending from the mountain into the valley. I will also have to accelerate to get up the mountain, and this will make my journey take longer than it would if the road was flat. Anyone who has driven a road like this knows that it quickly becomes physically and mentally tiring because of the great need for concentration.

Where I live, in New Jersey, I always need to watch for deer while I'm driving because they are known to suddenly run out into the road. Hitting a deer can cause serious injury to my car and possibly to me. (Unfortunately, I know this from personal experience.) It will delay me from reaching my destination. Likewise, if a road is very uneven or full of potholes, I am forced to drive more slowly and pay more attention to the road so I don't cause damage to my car. All these things can slow me down greatly.

By contrast, if the road has been properly prepared before me, my trip will go much more smoothly. With the right equipment, road crews can not only fill in potholes and flatten rough areas of road, but they can also excavate hills and valleys, so the road takes a much smoother and gentler route. This makes for not only a smoother and less stressful drive, but also a shorter trip. Good roads increase the speed and ease of travel in the natural. The same principle applies to our children's spiritual journeys. Our prayers open the door for God to work in their lives and prepare the way before them.

God wants our children's journeys to be blessed because He loves them. He wants the blessing on their lives to be a sign of His goodness and glory to the world.

A friend of mine recently told me a testimony of the power of her parents' prayers in her life. Growing up, her parents would pray with her every night before bed, and as part of that, they always prayed for her future husband. My friend's future husband grew up in a non-Christian family, but the hand of God was all over his life, protecting him from making bad decisions and going down destructive paths, even though other family members were involved in destructive patterns. He didn't know someone was praying for him every night, but the fruit of those prayers was evident. As a teen, he got saved during a dramatic encounter and has followed God ever since. When he eventually met his wife, they were both astounded to see how her parents' prayers for all those years had tangibly impacted his life and set him apart for God.

Powerful Parenting Insights

- Praying for our children's future spouses is crucial, as this is the second most important decision they will make in their lives (following their decision for Christ).
- We cannot overlook or underestimate the power of our prayers as parents.

The prayer focuses I have highlighted in these two chapters all go back to the essence of the gospel—which is holistic salvation in this life and in eternity. No matter where our children are in their journey, we can pray these prayers for them, as well as many others. These prayer points show us the overarching will of God for our children's lives, but we are not limited to just these. The Bible contains many promises we can pray over our children.

When I face a particular need or if I am not sure what to pray, I search for that subject in an online Bible concordance like Bible Gateway. Seeing what the Bible says about our children and the circumstances they face will build our faith. As we pray, God's power will be released, and Heaven will begin to come to earth in their lives.

Digging Deeper Workbook Chapter 18

Practical Prayers for Our Children Part Two

Based on what you learned in this chapter, write a prayer for each of these areas. Leave a blank where you can insert the name of the child (natural or spiritual) you are praying for.

Provision

And my God will meet all your needs according to the riches of his glory in Christ Jesus. (Philippians 4:19)

God wants to provide for your child in the natural. God has all the wisdom you need, and He wants to help you and your child thrive and prosper in all areas, including your finances.

Open Doors and Favor

Surely, LORD, you bless the righteous; you surround them with your favor as with a shield. (Psalm 5:12)

God wants to surround your child with the shield of His favor, which will protect them from attacks against their calling. Favor looks like miraculously being promoted to positions of authority within godless and evil kingdoms—without compromising their convictions or faith. This is what you want for your child as they pursue education, careers, athletics, and so forth.

Whatever calling God has given your child, you can assist them by praying God would open doors of favor so they can fulfill their calling.

When your child faces tough times, pray God would open a door of deliverance for them. He is able to open doors of deliverance, favor, and promotion for your child that no one can close.

Creative Minds

Pray God would strengthen and quicken your child's mind, so they have ease in learning, possess a good memory, and be creative and imaginative thinkers.

If your child struggles with anxiety, depression, or any other mental illness, claim the promise in 2 Timothy 1:7 and declare their mind is made whole and healthy by the blood of Jesus. The enemy wants to lie to them and cause their minds to turn against them, but the truth is that the Spirit of God has provided healing for their minds.

Whether your child is in school or in the workforce, pray God would strengthen their minds, give them creative ideas, and help them to focus and have an excellent memory.

Courage, Strength, and Peace

Pray your child will "be strong in the Lord and in his mighty power" (Ephesians 6:10).

Declare over _____ the promises of Hebrews 13:6—"The Lord is _____ helper; _____ will not be afraid. What can mere mortals do to _____," and Deuteronomy 31:6, "Be strong and courageous. Do not be afraid or terrified because of them, for the LORD your God goes with _____, he will never leave _____ nor forsake _____."

Pray your child would receive a revelation of God's peace and learn how to step into His peace in all circumstances.

Obedient Hearts

The older your child gets, the more you need to pray the Lord will lead them as they begin to make an increasing number of decisions independently. Pray your child would learn to discern the will of God and then choose to obey His will.

> *We continually ask God to fill you with the knowledge of his will through all the wisdom and understanding that the Spirit gives, so that you may live a life worthy of the Lord and please him in every way: bearing fruit in every good work, growing in the knowledge of God.* (Colossians 1:9–10)

> *His divine power has given us everything we need for a godly life through our knowledge of him who called us by his own glory and goodness.* (2 Peter 1:3)

Your child has what it takes to live righteously and to please God. They have the ability to succeed in this, but they also have the freedom to disobey. Thus, your prayer should be they would not only discern God's will, but also choose to follow it.

Manifestation of Destiny

Every child is born with a unique destiny and purpose on this earth. Part of your job as parents is to pray that destiny into being. Call forth your child's destiny and the good that is already inside them in Jesus' name.

Put your child's name in Psalm 139 and declare it aloud as a prophetic decree over their lives.

Pray your child would yield to their gifting from the womb and be true to their destiny.

Pray God the Father, the Master Potter would mold your child according to His will (see Jeremiah 18:1–6).

Jesus taught us to pray, "Our Father in heaven, hallowed be your name, your kingdom come, your will be done, on earth as it is in heaven" (Matthew 6:9–10). You can apply this to your child by praying that what God has ordained for them in Heaven would manifest on earth.

A Blessed Future

Praying for a blessed future for your child encompasses more than their calling in life. It includes all their life decisions and situations. You can prepare a way for your child in the Spirit through your prayers.

Spiritually prepare your child's heart to receive the truth of the Word of God (see Mark 4:1–20).

Declare straight paths, valleys raised up, mountains made low, and rough ground made smooth for them in the name of Jesus. Become laborers with God (see 2 Corinthians 6:1) to prepare the way for your child's success in life.

God loves your child and wants your child's journey to be blessed. Praying for your child's future spouse is crucial, as this is the second most important decision they will make in their lives.

Conclusion

As I worked on this book, in my mind's eye I saw many households where the enemy was lurking in the cracks and behind the doors wanting to come in. However, when he sees praying parents, he is afraid of what we might do. He is afraid we will bind him and cast him out. The devil goes about like a roaring lion, seeking people to devour (see 1 Peter 5:8), but though he roars, he has no teeth. Jesus forever knocked out his teeth when He defeated him in His death and resurrection.

I saw how afraid he is of us. He trembles at the thought that we would stand on the Word of God and ask God to perform His will on behalf of our children. This is good news!

It is time for us to arise. We have everything we need to be the spiritual leaders in our homes. Let us take back what the enemy has stolen. Our children are our heritage—gifts from the heart of the Father. Boldly and strongly, we must stand in the gap for them. When we do, we will see God do exceedingly, abundantly above all we could ask, hope, dream, or desire in their lives (see Ephesians 3:20).

As praying parents, we are building our families on the solid foundation of the Word of God. We are like the builder Jesus talked about, whose house withstood the torrential storm:

> *Therefore everyone who hears these words of mine and puts them into practice is like a wise man who built his house on the rock. The rain came down, the streams*

> *rose, and the winds blew and beat against that house; yet it did not fall, because it had its foundation on the rock.* (Matthew 7:24–25)

Through faith-filled prayer, we are building our house upon the rock. The winds may blow and the storms may come, but as praying parents, we can abort the plans of the enemy. Our family structures will not sink because they are built upon faith in God's Word. Even those of us who did not raise our children in the things of God can change all of that by becoming praying parents now. Our prayers and the testimony of our lives will draw our children to God!

It may take time, but if we do not give up, we cannot fail. Every prayer we pray is like a seed. It never dies. Even if it is hidden under the soil for many years, it is still there, waiting to come to life. All the prayers we have ever prayed for our children are eternal. Long after we have left this earth, our prayers will continue to produce on behalf of our children. Even Jesus prayed prayers that are still in the process of coming to pass (see John 17). We can leave a rich spiritual inheritance to our children by becoming intercessors for them (see Proverbs 13:22).

The evidence and the invitation are clear. Let's start today to pray purposefully and persistently for our children. The total fruit of our prayers can only be measured in eternity. When we get there, we will be amazed by all God has done in our families through our simple prayers.

Appendix 1

More Sample Prayers

Prayer for a Child

Father, I pray _____ would be strengthened and reinforced with mighty power in his/her inner being by the Holy Spirit. May Christ through faith actually dwell (settle down, abide, make His permanent home) in his/her heart! May _____ be rooted deeply in love and founded securely on love, so that he/she may have the power and strength to grasp the experience of that love—what is the breadth and length and height and depth of it. I pray _____ may really come to know practically, through experience for him/herself the love of Christ, which far surpasses mere human knowledge and reasoning. I pray _____ would be filled through all his/her being with all the fullness of God and have the richest measure of Your divine Presence.

I pray _____ will be filled with the knowledge of Your will in all wisdom and understanding. I pray his/her walk would be worthy of You, fully pleasing You and fruitful in every good work. May he/she increase in the knowledge of You and be strengthened with all might, according to Your glorious power, for all patience and long suffering with joy. May he/she give thanks to You who has qualified him/her to be a partaker of the inheritance of the saints in the light. You have delivered _____ from the power of darkness and conveyed him/

her into the Kingdom of the Son of Your love, in whom he/she has redemption through His blood, the forgiveness of sins.

I release my faith and declare, Father, that as _____ grows in grace and in the knowledge of our Lord Jesus Christ, he/she will not depart from the faith or from the things he/she has been taught. I pray that every word of God that has been sown into his/her heart will not return void, but will sprout and bring forth abundant fruit in _____'s life. I agree that the Word of God will not depart out of _____'s mouth, but he/she will love Your Word and meditate in it day and night and will observe to do according to all that is written in it. Lord God, I thank You that You will make _____'s way prosperous, and he/she will have good success.

Father, I pray _____ would successfully run the race set before him/her. May _____ not look to anything but You, the Author and Finisher of his/her faith. I speak to the weights, the sins, and the distractions that would endeavor to slow _____ down, and I say, "Be removed in the name of Jesus!" I speak to any spirits of fear, anxiety, worry, or suicide and command you to release _____ and stay far from him/her.

Our Father, I pray _____ would be motivated by Your plans and what You have called him/her to be and do. I pray _____ would not lean on his/her own understanding or what society says, but I pray _____ would sense destiny within him/her calling him/her. I speak to the destiny within _____ to come forth in the name of Jesus! I command the blinders to come off of his/her eyes in the name of Jesus. Destiny, arise and come forth! Holy Spirit, Spirit of Truth, please help _____ in this day and hour. Convict and convince _____ of his/her need for Jesus and fill him/her with the desire to serve Jesus as Lord all the days of his/her life.

Holy Spirit, I ask You to manifest Yourself wherever _____ goes. Warn him/her also of impending danger so that he/she will stay away from those things that would steal, kill, or destroy his/her destiny. May You rise up within _____ and pour Your Spirit out so much upon _____ that he/she will cry out to You in his/her time of need. May _____ long for You as the psalmist David did when he found himself in a dry and thirsty land. I agree that _____ will see Your power and Your glory, Father. Abba Father, show Yourself strong to him/her.

Finally, Father, I declare that _____ is strong in You and in the power of Your might. _____ will put on the whole armor of God so that he/she may stand against the devil. _____ has girded his/her waist with truth, put on the breastplate of righteousness, and has his/her feet shod with the gospel of peace. Above all, _____ takes the shield of faith, with which he/she will be able to quench all the fiery darts of the wicked one. Give _____ the wisdom to discern what is good and what is evil. I declare that he/she takes the helmet of salvation and the sword of the Spirit, which is the Word of God.

Father, I ask that he/she would always desire to pray in the Spirit. Holy Spirit, spirit of grace and supplication, I ask that You would stir within _____ a deep hunger for intimacy with Jesus in the secret place of prayer, that he/she would prioritize the best part of being a believer, which is knowing Jesus. May he/she every day become more deeply and intimately acquainted with Jesus. I agree with You, Father, that _____ will not get spiritually bored. Instead, I ask that You would surprise him/her with joy and fun in Your presence. I ask that You would reveal Your heart to _____, wherever he/she is at this moment, in the nighttime, in the day, and when he/she reads the Bible or attends church. May he/she be continually aware of Your presence with him/her.

A Prayer for the Rising Generations

Father, I see an army of young men and women rising in this hour. Soldiers—men and woman who are armed and dangerous to the kingdom of darkness. May You anoint them with fresh oil more than any other generation. You said in Your Word that where sin abounds Your grace abounds so much more, so I ask for abundance of grace, abundance of signs and wonders and miracles to be manifest to this generation. As a natural/spiritual parent, I agree with Your will that not one of them would be lost, but all of them would be saved and come to the knowledge of the truth.

I release my faith Father, and I refuse to be moved by temporal circumstances. I release my faith now into the atmosphere, and I call every lost and prodigal son and daughter home in the name of Jesus. For those who walk with You and have clean hands and pure hearts—I ask You to bless them with wisdom and spiritual understanding. May they see and hear with revelation from the Holy Spirit. May the eyes of their understanding be enlightened so they may know what You have called them to do and be as they live temporarily on this earth.

I pray that this generation of young people would become a body wholly filled and flooded with You! I pray that this generation would rise up and call their parents blessed for training them in the way they should go. I pray that our children and youth would be a generation who, like the first-century believers, turns the world upside down with the gospel. May our children turn the world upside down with the flames of a revival spirit. May the river of God rise up from within them, like an artesian well, so much that they won't be able to contain the river arising in their hearts. I pray that from this river would come a greater measure of boldness, that they would open their mouths boldly and make known the mystery of the gospel to their generation. I break the spirit of fear and intimidation that would keep them from announcing their faith to their peers in Jesus' name.

May the light of the glory of God rise within the youth of this nation. May they be radiant and give You the glory. May they shine as lights in the darkness. May their light shine so brightly that their unbelieving peers will be drawn to You, Father. May their light shine so brightly that their peers will see Jesus and come to the knowledge of the truth. I bind every work of darkness that would put a stronghold on this generation of believers and the young budding leaders. No weapon formed against our youth shall prosper, in the name of Jesus. I declare that our youth have strength for all things in Christ, who empowers them. They are ready for anything and equal to any task, because Christ infuses them with His strength on the inside. They are self-sufficient in Christ's sufficiency. They will do above and beyond all we can ask or imagine—performing greater works than Jesus did for the glory of God!

Appendix 2
Bible Promises for Our Children

Here is a list of powerful promises that we can pray and declare over our children. The Bible contains many more promises than just these few pages, but these are a good place to start.

Genesis 9:9— *I now establish my covenant with you and with your descendants after you.*

Genesis 17:7— *I will establish my covenant as an everlasting covenant between me and you and your descendants after you for the generations to come, to be your God and the God of your descendants after you.*

Genesis 28:3–4— *May God Almighty bless you and make you fruitful and increase your numbers until you become a community of peoples. May he give you and your descendants the blessing given to Abraham, so that you may take possession of the land where you now reside as a foreigner, the land God gave to Abraham.*

Exodus 23:26— *And none will miscarry or be barren in your land. I will give you a full life span.*

Numbers 23:19— *God is not human, that he should lie, not a human being, that he should change His mind. Does He speak and then not act? Does He promise and not fulfill?*

Deuteronomy 7:14— *You will be blessed more than any other people; none of your men or women will be childless, nor will any of your livestock be without young.*

Deuteronomy 28:4— *The fruit of your womb will be blessed, and the crops of your land and the young of your livestock—the calves of your herds and the lambs of your flocks.*

Deuteronomy 30:6— *The Lord your God will circumcise your hearts and the hearts of your descendants, so that you may love him with all your heart and with all your soul, and live.*

Psalm 1:1–3— *Blessed is the one who does not walk in step with the wicked or stand in the way that sinners take or sit in the company of mockers, but whose delight is in the law of the Lord, and who meditates on his law day and night. That person is like a tree planted by streams of water, which yields its fruit in season and whose leaf does not wither—whatever they do prospers.*

Psalm 4:8— *In peace I will lie down and sleep, for you alone, Lord, make me dwell in safety.*

Psalm 9:9— *The Lord is a refuge for the oppressed, a stronghold in times of trouble.*

Psalm 25:12–13— *Who, then, are those who fear the Lord? He will instruct them in the ways they should choose. They will spend their days in prosperity, and their descendants will inherit the land.*

Psalm 37:25— *I was young and now I am old, yet I have never seen the righteous forsaken for their children begging bread.*

Psalm 72:4— *May he defend the afflicted among the people and save the children of the needy; may he crush the oppressor.*

Psalm 78:1–4— *My people, hear my teaching; listen to the words of my mouth. I will open my mouth with a parable; I will utter hidden things, things from of old—things we have heard and known, things our ancestors have told us. We will not hide them from their descendants; we will tell the next generation the praiseworthy deeds of the Lord, his power, and the wonders he has done.*

Psalm 90:16— *May your deeds be shown to your servants, your splendor to their children.*

Psalm 91— *Whoever dwells in the shelter of the Most High will rest in the shadow of the Almighty. I will say of the Lord, "He is my refuge and my fortress, my God, in whom I trust." Surely he will save you from the fowler's snare and from the deadly pestilence. He will cover you with his feathers, and under his wings you will find refuge; his faithfulness will be your shield and rampart. You will not fear the terror of night, nor the arrow that flies by day, nor the pestilence that stalks in the darkness, nor the plague that destroys at midday. A thousand may fall at your side, ten thousand at your right hand, but it will not come near you. You will only observe with your eyes and see the punishment of the wicked. If you say, "The Lord is my refuge," and you make the Most High your dwelling, no harm will overtake you, no disaster will come near your tent. For he will command his angels concerning you to guard you in all your ways; they will lift you up in their hands, so that you will not strike your foot against a stone. You will tread on the lion and the cobra; you will trample the great lion and the serpent. "Because he loves me," says the Lord, "I will rescue* him; I will protect him, for he acknowledges my name. He will call on me, and I will answer him; I will be with him in trouble, I will deliver him and honor him. With long life I will satisfy him and show him my salvation."

Psalm 92:14— *They will still bear fruit in old age, they will stay fresh and green.*

Psalm 103:17–19— *But from everlasting to everlasting the* LORD's *love is with those who fear him, and his righteousness with their children's children—with those who keep his covenant and remember to obey his precepts. The* LORD *has established his throne in heaven, and his kingdom rules over all.*

Psalm 112:2— *Their children will be mighty in the land; the generation of the upright will be blessed.*

Psalm 113:9— *He settles the childless woman in her home as a happy mother of children.*

Psalm 127:3–5— *Children are a heritage from the* LORD, *offspring a reward from him. Like arrows in the hands of a warrior are children born in one's youth. Blessed is the man whose quiver is full of them. They will not be put to shame when they contend with their opponents in court.*

Psalm 128:3— *Your wife will be like a fruitful vine within your house; your children will be like olive shoots around your table.*

Psalm 128:6— *May you live to see your children's children.*

Psalm 144:12— *Then our sons in their youth will be like well-nurtured plants, and our daughters will be like pillars carved to adorn a palace.*

Psalm 147:13— *He strengthens the bars of your gates and blesses your people within you.*

Proverbs 3:5–6— *Trust in the Lord with all your heart and lean not on your own understanding; in all your ways submit to him, and he will make your paths straight.*

Proverbs 4:5–7— *Get wisdom, get understanding; do not forget my words or turn away from them. Do not forsake wisdom, and she will protect you; love her, and she will watch over you. The beginning of wisdom is this: Get wisdom. Though it cost all you have, get understanding.*

Proverbs 9:10–12— *The fear of the Lord is the beginning of wisdom, and knowledge of the Holy One is understanding. For through wisdom your days will be many, and years will be added to your life. If you are wise, your wisdom will reward you; if you are a mocker, you alone will suffer.*

Proverbs 10:22— *The blessing of the Lord brings wealth, without painful toil for it.*

Proverbs 11:21— *Be sure of this: The wicked will not go unpunished, but those who are righteous will go free.*

Proverbs 12:26— *The righteous choose their friends carefully, but the way of the wicked leads them astray.*

Proverbs 14:26— *Whoever fears the Lord has a secure fortress, and for their children it will be a refuge.*

Proverbs 17:6— *Children's children are a crown to the aged, and parents are the pride of their children.*

Proverbs 20:7— *The righteous lead blameless lives; blessed are their children after them.*

Proverbs 22:5–6— *In the paths of the wicked are snares and pitfalls, but those who would preserve their life stay far from them. Start children off on the way they should go, and even when they are old they will not turn from it.*

Proverbs 31:28— *Her children arise and call her blessed; her husband also, and he praises her.*

Isaiah 8:18— *Here am I, and the children the Lord has given me. We are signs and symbols in Israel from the Lord Almighty, who dwells on Mount Zion.*

Isaiah 11:2–3— *The Spirit of the Lord will rest on him— the Spirit of wisdom and of understanding, the Spirit of counsel and of might, the Spirit of the knowledge and fear of the Lord— and he will delight in the fear of the Lord. He will not judge by what he sees with his eyes, or decide by what he hears with his ears.*

Isaiah 49:25— *But this is what the Lord says: "Yes, captives will be taken from warriors, and plunder retrieved from the fierce; I will contend with those who contend with you, and your children I will save."*

Isaiah 54:13— *All your children will be taught by the Lord, and great will be their peace.*

Isaiah 55:2— *Why spend money on what is not bread, and your labor on what does not satisfy? Listen, listen to me, and eat what is good, and you will delight in the richest of fare.*

Isaiah 63:4— *It was for me the day of vengeance; the year for me to redeem had come.*

Isaiah 65:23— *They will not labor in vain, nor will they bear children doomed to misfortune; for they will be a people blessed by the* Lord, *they and their descendants with them.*

Jeremiah 1:5— *Before I formed you in the womb I knew you, before you were born I set you apart; I appointed you as a prophet to the nations.*

Jeremiah 24:7 "…*I will give them a heart to know Me, that I am the Lord; and they shall be My people, and I will be their God, for they shall return to Me with their whole heart.*"

Jeremiah 29:11— "*For I know the plans I have for you,*" *declares the* Lord, "*plans to prosper you and not to harm you, plans to give you hope and a future.*"

Jeremiah 31:16–17— *This is what the* Lord *says:* "*Restrain your voice from weeping and your eyes from tears, for your work will be rewarded,*" *declares the* Lord. "*They will return from the land of the enemy. So there is hope for your descendants,*" *declares the* Lord. "*Your children will return to their own land.*"

Jeremiah 32:38–40— *They will be my people, and I will be their God. I will give them singleness of heart and action, so that they will always fear me and that all will then go well for them and for their children after them. I will make an everlasting covenant with them: I will never stop doing good to them, and I will inspire them to fear me, so that they will never turn away from me.*

Jeremiah 33:3— *Call to me and I will answer you and tell you great and unsearchable things you do not know.*

Lamentations 2:19— *Arise, cry out in the night, as the watches of the night begin; pour out your heart like water in the presence of the Lord. Lift up your hands to him for the lives of your children, who faint from hunger at every street corner.*

Joel 2:28— *I will pour out my Spirit on all people. Your sons and daughters will prophesy, your old men will dream dreams, your young men will see visions.*

Zephaniah 3:19— *At that time I will deal with all who oppressed you. I will rescue the lame; I will gather the exiles. I will give them praise and honor in every land where they have suffered shame.*

Mathew 19:26— *Jesus looked at them and said, "With man this is impossible, but with God all things are possible."*

John 10:10— *The thief comes only to steal and kill and destroy; I have come that they may have life, and have it to the full.*

Acts 16:31— *Believe in the Lord Jesus, and you will be saved—you and your household.*

Romans 5:20— *But where sin increased, grace increased all the more.*

2 Corinthians 1:20— *For no matter how many promises God has made, they are "Yes" in Christ. And so through him the "Amen" is spoken by us to the glory of God.*

Philippians 1:6— *Being confident of this, that he who began a good work in you will carry it on to completion until the day of Christ Jesus.*

James 1:5— *If any of you lacks wisdom, you should ask God, who gives generously to all without finding fault, and it will be given to you.*

Endnotes

1 See Chapter 2 for a more in-depth explanation on God's heart and Kingdom plan for families.
2 See Chapter 2 for a more in-depth explanation on God's heart and Kingdom plan for families.
3 www.merriam-webster.com
4 *Boundaries with Kids* by Cloud and Townsend; *Parenting with Love and Logic* by Foster Cline, and *Loving Our Kids on Purpose* by Danny Silk are all great resources on parenting and boundaries.
5
6 *Strong's Exhaustive Concordance*, s.v. "Parrhesia," Greek #3954.
7 From the New International Translation
8 Micah Solomon, "2015 Is the Year of the Millennial Customer: 5 Key Traits These 80 Million Consumers Share" (December 29, 2014); https://www.forbes.com/sites/micahsolomon/2014/12/29/5-traits-that-define-the-80-million-millennial-customers-coming-your-way/#7e6ae77825e5 (accessed April 19, 2017).
9 Tom Agan, "Embracing the Millennials' Mind-set at Work," *New York Times* (November 9, 2013); http://www.nytimes.com/2013/11/10/jobs/embracing-the-millennials-mind-set-at-work.html (accessed April 19, 2017).
10 Tom Agan, "Embracing the Millennials' Mind-set at Work," *New York Times* (November 9, 2013); http://www.nytimes.com/2013/11/10/jobs/embracing-the-millennials-mind-set-at-work.html (accessed April 19, 2017).
11 Ibid.

12 Alissa Wilkinson, "After Columbine, Martyrdom Became a Powerful Fantasy for Christian Teenagers," (April 20, 2017); http://www.vox.com/culture/2017/4/20/15369442/columbine-anniversary-cassie-bernall-rachel-scott-martyrdom (accessed April 24, 2017).

13 Alex Williams, "Move Over Millennials, Here Comes Generation Z," *New York Times* (September 18, 2015); https://www.nytimes.com/2015/09/20/fashion/move-over-millennials-here-comes-generation-z.html?_r=0 (accessed April 18, 2017).

14 Ron Alsop, *The Trophy Kids Grow Up: How the Millennial Generation is Shaking Up the Workplace* (San Francisco, CA: Jossey-Bass, 2008).

15 Dan Schawbel, "Millennials vs. Baby Boomers: Who Would You Rather Hire?" *Time* (March 29, 2012); http://business.time.com/2012/03/29/millennials-vs-baby-boomers-who-would-you-rather-hire/ (accessed April 13, 2017).

16 Josh Sanburn, "Millennials: The Next Greatest Generation?" *Time* (May 9, 2013); http://nation.time.com/2013/05/09/millennials-the-next-greatest-generation/ (accessed April 13, 2017).

17 "How Millennial Trophies Created a Generation of Workaholics," *The Atlantic*; http://www.theatlantic.com/sponsored/project-time-off/how-millennial-trophies-created-a-generation-of-workaholics/1260/?utm_source=eb (accessed April 24, 2017).

18 "How Millennial Trophies Created a Generation of Workaholics," *The Atlantic*; http://www.theatlantic.com/sponsored/project-time-off/how-millennial-trophies-created-a-generation-of-workaholics/1260/?utm_source=eb (accessed April 24, 2017).

19 Tim Elmore, "Six Defining Characteristics of Generation Z," (September 3, 2015); https://growingleaders.com/blog/six-defining-characteristics-of-generation-z/ (accessed April 19, 2017).

20 Alex Williams, "Move Over Millennials, Here Comes Generation Z," *New York Times* (September 18, 2015); https://www.nytimes.com/2015/09/20/fashion/move-over-millennials-here-comes-generation-z.html?_r=0 (accessed April 18, 2017).

21 Theo Priestley, "Why the Next Generation After Millennials Will Be Builders, Not Founders," (December 30, 2015); https://www.forbes.com/sites/theopriestley/2015/12/30/

why-the-next-generation-after-millennials-will-be-builders-not-founders/#4ddda2425ccb (accessed April 19, 2017).
22   Ibid.
23   Dr. Caroline Leaf, *Switch on Your Brain* (Grand Rapids, MI: Baker Books, 2013), 95.
24   Ibid., 96.
25   Leaf, 97.
26   Ibid., 96.
27   Ibid.
28   Ibid., 97.
29   Joel Stein, "Millennials: The Me Me Generation," *Time* (May 20, 2013); http://time.com/247/millennials-the-me-me-me-generation/ (accessed April 19, 2017).
30   Susanna Scrobsdorff, "Teen Depression and Anxiety: Why the Kids Are Not Alright" (October 27, 2016); http://time.com/4547322/american-teens-anxious-depressed-overwhelmed/ (accessed April 13, 2016).
31   http://ignitinghope.com.
32   "Dutch Sheets Word of the Lord 2017," *YouTube* (January 14, 2017), minute 53; https://www.youtube.com/watch?v=vewokqJx-Bl8&sns=em (accessed December 6, 2017).
33   "Religion Among the Millennials," *Pew Research Center* (February 17, 2010); http://www.pewforum.org/2010/02/17/religion-among-the-millennials/ (accessed April 27, 2017).
34   Ann Byle, "Charismatic Millennials Spreading the Fame of Jesus," *Charisma Magazine* (August 16, 2015); http://www.charismamag.com/anniversary/anniversary/23811-spreading-the-fame-of-jesus (accessed April 27, 2017).
35   http://ignitinghope.com.
36   Karl Moore, "Authenticity: The Way to the Millennial's Heart" *Forbes* (August 14, 2014); https://www.forbes.com/sites/karlmoore/2014/08/14/authenticity-the-way-to-the-millennials-heart/#abc81e645317 (accessed April 28, 2017).
37   Colby B. Jubenville, "Millennials Prefer the Real Deal" *The Washington Times* (November 9, 2016); http://www.washingtontimes.com/

news/2016/nov/9/millennials-prefer-authenticity/ (accessed April 28, 2017).

38 Jason Upton, "Lion of Judah," *Dying Star*, music CD (Key of David Ministries, 2002).

39 Johnson, *When Heaven Invades Earth* (Shippensburg, PA: Treasure House, 2003), 23.

40 Bill Johnson, "How to Pray and Decree," *YouTube* (published June 8, 2016); https://www.youtube.com/watch?v=NdUzAMVnc4Y (accessed May 4, 2017).

41 Peter Guirguis, "Top 5 Reasons Why Internet Evangelism Is the Next Big Thing," *Not Ashamed of the Gospel* (April 16, 2012); http://notashamedofthegospel.com/online-evangelism-101/top-5-reasons-why-internet-evangelism-is-the-next-big-thing/ (accessed May 4, 2017).

42 Ed Stetzer, "3 Ways Technology Enables the Mission of the Church," *Christianity Today* (October 27, 2014); http://www.christianity-today.com/edstetzer/2014/october/3-ways-technology-enables-mission-of-church.html (accessed May 9, 2017).

43 Stormie Omartian, *The Power of a Praying Parent* (Eugene, OR: Harvest House Publishers, 2014), 39.

44 Oswald Chambers, quoted in Mark Water, Ed., *Encyclopedia of Prayer and Praise* (Peabody, MA: Hendrickson Publishers, 2004), 1136.

45 Mark Batterson, *Praying Circles around Your Children* (Grand Rapids, MI: Zondervan, 2012), 11.

46 Dr. Caroline Leaf, *Switch on Your Brain* (Grand Rapids, MI: Baker Books, 2013), 110.

47 Leaf, 110–111.

48 Leaf, 111.

49 E.M. Bounds, quoted in Mark Water, Ed., *Encyclopedia of Prayer and Praise* (Peabody, MA: Hendrickson Publishers, 2004), 1126.

50 Leaf, 115.

51 I recommend the Myers-Briggs personality test, which also offers a test to assess children. Find out more information at http://www.myers-briggs.org/my-mbti-personality-type/take-the-mbti-instrument.

52 I recommend the Myers-Briggs personality test, which also offers a test to assess children. Find out more information at http://www.myers-briggs.org/my-mbti-personality-type/take-the-mbti-instrument.
53 In Appendix 2, I have included a list of verses I often pray over my children. These are a great place to start in learning to pray the Bible. I also talk about specific prayers that we can pray for our children according to the general will of God as revealed in the Bible.
54 Arthur Wallis, *Pray in the Spirit* (Fort Washington, PA: CLC Ministries, 2005), 30.
55 Arthur Wallis, *Pray in the Spirit* (Fort Washington, PA: CLC Ministries, 2005), 22.
56 James Goll, "Travail: The Prayer that Brings Birth," *Elijah List* (Jan 21, 2005); http://www.elijahlist.com/words/display_word/2791 (accessed Dec 6, 2017).
57 Arthur Wallis, *Pray in the Spirit* (Fort Washington, PA: CLC Ministries, 2005), 90.
58 In Appendix 2, I have included a list of verses I often pray over my children. These are a great place to start in learning to pray the Bible. I also talk about specific prayers that we can pray for our children according to the general will of God as revealed in the Bible.
59 Bill Johnson, *Hosting the Presence Workbook: Unveiling Heaven's Agenda* (Shippensburg, PA: Destiny Image, 2013), 21. Used with permission.
60 Steve Backlund, "Hope," *Igniting Hope Ministries*; http://ignitinghope.com/hope (accessed August 3, 2017).
61 God first told Abraham he would be the father of many nations when He told him to leave his homeland. Abraham was 75 years old. Fifteen years later, when Abraham was 90, God renewed His promise that they would have a son. Ten years later, when Abraham was 100, Sarah finally gave birth to Isaac. They waited twenty-five years in faith.
62 Vine's Complete Expository Dictionary, ©1984,1996, Thomas Nelson, Inc., Nashville, TN.
63 I recommend Gary Smally's book, *The Key to Your Child's Heart*. It is tremendously helpful in teaching us how to give love to our children in their own love language.

CPSIA information can be obtained
at www.ICGtesting.com
Printed in the USA
LVHW042105300622
722480LV00005B/730